Math in Fables & Myths
Solving Word Problems & Readers' Theatre

By Nancy Polette
and
Joan Ebbesmeyer

Published by Pieces of Learning
© 2005 Polette, Ebbesmeyer
CLC0345
ISBN 978-1-931334-58-7
Graphic Production by Sharolyn Hill

www.piecesoflearning.com

All rights reserved. In our effort to produce high quality educational products we offer portions of this book as "reproducible." Permission is granted, therefore, to the buyer - one teacher - to reproduce student activity pages in LIMITED quantities for students in the buyer's classroom only. The right to reproduce is not extended to other teachers, entire schools, or to school systems. Use of any pages on the Internet is strictly forbidden. No other part of this publication may be reproduced in whole or part. The whole publication may not be stored in a retrieval system, or transmitted in any form or by any means, electronic, mechanical, photocopying, recording, or otherwise without written permission of the publisher.
For any other use contact Pieces of Learning at 1-800-729-5137.
For a complete catalog of products contact Pieces of Learning
or visit our Web Site at www.piecesoflearning.com

Math in Fables & Myths

Table of Contents

Introduction 5

Standards 6

Addition
The Wolf, the Nanny Goat and the Kid 9
The Milkmaid and her Pail 11

Subtraction
The Man, the Boy and the Donkey 13
The Lion and the Mouse 14

Addition, Subtraction
Belling the Cat 16

Multiplication
The Hare and the Tortoise 19
The Fox and the Goat 21

Addition, Subtraction, Multiplication
The Grasshopper and the Ants 23

Division
The Boy Who Cried Wolf 25
The Town Mouse and the Country
Mouse 27

Multiplication, Division
A Wolf in Sheep's Clothing 29

Addition, Subtraction, Multiplication, Division
Cinderella 32
The Golden Goose 36

Fractions
The Tower of the Dragon 39
Hansel & Gretel 45

Decimals and Percents
The Fisherman and His Wife 50

Putting It All Together
Grades 3-4
Hermes, The Merry Olympian 54
The Story of Daphne and Apollo 59

Grade 4
Odysseus and the Cyclops 65

Grades 4-5
Ceyx and Halcyone 75

Grade 4
The Queen of the Dead 79

Grade 5
Daedalus, The Bird Man 87
Chariot of the Sun 94
Athena and the Weaving Contest 101
The Magnificent Maze of Minos 107

Answers 114-118

INTRODUCTION

Word problems can be no problem at all when young thespians get to work on them!

By using addition skills, beginning problem solvers can save the little goat from the hungry wolf at the door. As Mr. Whiskers and the Mouse Mayor debate how to save the mice from the cat, subtraction easily solves the problem. How can tortoise win the race with hare? By using multiplication, of course.

Each of the 25 plays requires the solving of word problems that become part of the play script to perform. Each new play introduces additional math operations in a progressive sequence. The first play requires only basic knowledge of addition. The final play in the series requires knowledge of fractions, reciprocals, mean, median, working with data and simple geometry.

Here are plays that will motivate students to use the math skills they have learned in a creative way. Students can perform plays for the class, for other classes, or for the whole school. Audience members will see that math is an essential part of everyday life and that knowledge of math can be very valuable in solving everyday problems.

The math operations in the plays are based on the national standards for grades 3 through 6:
- addition
- subtraction
- multiplication
- division
- fractions
- decimals
- percents
- one- and two-step problems
- metrics
- measurement
- Roman numerals
- opposite operations
- variables
- rates and speed
- averages
- ratio
- reciprocals
- mean
- median
- and beginning geometry

As students visit the tower of the dragon, rescue Hansel and Gretel, travel with Odysseus to confont the monster Cyclops, fly with Daedalus the bird man, and find their way out of the magnificent maze of Minos..all by using math skills . . . they will discover that **MATH HAS NEVER BEEN SO MUCH FUN!**

MATHEMATICS CONCEPTS AND SKILLS
Based on National Standards

1. Number Sense

A. Use real-life experiences, physical materials, and technology to construct meanings for numbers.

B. Whole numbers through millions.

C. Commonly used fractions as part of a whole and as a subset of a set.

D. Decimals through hundredths.

E. Demonstrate an understanding of place value concepts.

F. Demonstrate a sense of the relative magnitudes of numbers.

G. Understand the various uses of numbers. Counting, measuring, labeling, locating.

H. Use concrete and pictorial models to relate whole numbers, commonly used fractions, and decimals to each other, and to represent equivalent forms of the same number.

I. Compare and order numbers.

J. Explore settings that give rise to negative numbers: temperatures below 0, debts.

2. Numerical Operations

A. Develop the meanings of the four basic arithmetic operations by modeling a large variety of problems.

B. Addition and subtraction: joining, separating, comparing.

C. Multiplication: repeated addition, area/array.

D. Division: repeated subtraction, sharing.

E. Use efficient and accurate pencil-and-paper procedures for computation with whole numbers. (Addition, subtraction, multiplication, division).

F. Division of 4-5 digit numbers by 2-3 digit numbers.

G. Construct and use procedures for performing decimal addition and subtraction.

H. Count and perform computations with money.

I. Check the reasonableness of results of computations.

J. Use concrete models to explore addition and subtraction with fractions.

K. Understand and use the inverse relationships between addition and subtraction and between multiplication and division.

3. Estimation
A. Judge without counting whether a set of objects has less than, more than, or the same number of objects as a reference set.
B. Construct and use a variety of estimation strategies (e.g., rounding and mental math) for estimating both quantities and the results of computations.
C. Recognize when an estimate is appropriate, and understand the usefulness of an estimate as distinct from an exact answer.
D. Use estimation to determine whether the result of a computation (either by calculator or by hand) is reasonable.

4. Work with data in the context of real-world situations by:
A. Formulating questions that lead to data collection and analysis.
B. Determining what data to collect and when and how to collect them.
C. Collecting, organizing, and displaying data.
D. Drawing reasonable conclusions based on data.

5. Measurement
A. Recognize and describe measurable attributes, such as length, liquid capacity, time, weight (mass), temperature, volume, monetary value, and angle size, and identify the appropriate unit to measure them.
B. Demonstrate understanding of basic facts, principles, and techniques of measurement, including
   * appropriate use of standard units (metric and U.S. Customary).
   * appropriate use and conversion of units within a system (such as yards, feet, and inches; kilograms and grams; gallons, quarts, pints, and cups).
   * judging the reasonableness of an obtained measurement as it relates to prior experience and familiar benchmarks.
C. Read and interpret measuring instruments (e.g., rulers, clocks, thermometers).

D. Determine measurements directly by using standard tools to these suggested degrees of accuracy
   * length to the nearest half-inch or nearest cm.
   * weight (mass) to the nearest ounce or nearest 5 grams.
   * temperature to the nearest 5.
   * time to the nearest minute.
   * monetary value to dollars and cents.
   * liquid capacity to the nearest fluid ounce.

6. **Problem Solving**
A. In problem-solving situations involving whole numbers, fractions and decimals select and efficiently use appropriate computational procedures such as
   * recalling the basic facts of addition, subtraction, multiplication, and division.
   * using decimals and fractions.
   * estimation.
   * selecting and applying algorithms for addition, subtraction, multiplication, and division.
B. Use reasoning abilities to
   * perceive patterns.
   * identify relationships.
   * formulate questions for further exploration.
   * justify strategies.
   * test reasonableness of results.

Addition

The Wolf, the Nanny Goat, and The Kid

Reading Parts: Narrator One, Narrator Two, Nanny Goat, Little Kid, Wolf

(1) Narrator One: A Nanny goat went out to fill her empty milk bags. She would get two bags filled at the red barn, two bags filled at the green barn, and one bag filled at the blue barn. She would bring _____ bags of milk home.

(2) Nanny Goat: I am locking the door, Little Kid. Do not open the door unless you are told this password: 'Beware of the wolf.' It is 12 miles to the red barn, 6 miles to the green barn and 6 miles to the blue barn. From the blue barn I will walk another 12 miles to get home. I will be tired for I will have walked _____ miles.

(3) Wolf: Nanny Goat does not know I am listening outside her door. I know what the password is. I will wait until she has been gone 20 minutes. Then I will wait another fifteen minutes to be sure she is not coming back. In just _____ minutes I will knock on the door.

(4) Narrator Two: While wolf was waiting to knock on the door, Little Goat was hungry. He found a bowl of strawberries and counted 32 strawberries in the bowl. He found another bowl of strawberries and counted 42 strawberries in the bowl. He ate all _____ strawberries.

(5) Wolf: I have waited long enough. I will knock on the door seven times, BANG, BANG, BANG, BANG, BANG, BANG, BANG. No one answers. I will knock on the door twelve times, BANG, BANG, BANG, BANG, BANG, BANG, BANG, BANG, BANG, BANG, BANG, BANG. My paw hurts from all this knocking. I have knocked a total of ___ times.

Work Space

© 2005 Polette, Ebbesmeyer   CLC0345 Pieces of Learning

The Wolf, the Nanny Goat, and The Kid

(6) Little Kid: Go away. It will take my mother two hours to walk to the red barn. One hour to walk from the red barn to the green barn and one hour to walk from the green barn to the blue barn. It will take another two hours to walk home from the blue barn. That is a total of _____ hours. She has only been gone a few minutes. It cannot be her at the door.

Wolf: I will say the password in a high voice: 'Beware the wolf!' Now, Little Kid, open the door.

(7) Little Kid: I will peek out the two east windows, the three west windows, and the four north windows. I have peeked out _____ windows but I cannot see you. I will let you in if you show me your white paw.

(8) Narrator One: Now everyone knows that wolves do not have white paws. Wolf thought and thought of what to do. He scratched his right ear and thought for five minutes. He scratched his left ear and thought for ten minutes. He scratched his nose and thought for fifteen minutes. He thought and thought for a total of _____ minutes.

(9) Wolf: I could climb up 25 feet to the top of the house and climb 25 feet down the chimney. I would travel a total of _____ feet. That is too much climbing. I will go home.

All: And that is just what he did. It is better to be sure than to be sorry.

Work Space

The Wolf, the Nanny Goat, and The Kid
Answers are on page 114

Addition

The Milkmaid and Her Pail

Reading Parts: Narrator, Milkmaid

Work Space

(1) Narrator: A farmer's daughter was carrying her pail of milk from the field to the farmhouse. She would need to take 23 steps to the fence, 38 steps to the gate and 216 steps to the farmhouse. Walking with the pail on her head she would take _____ steps to arrive at the farmhouse.

(2) Milkmaid: When I sell the milk in this pail I can buy 200 eggs. Fifty brown eggs will cost $1.44; 100 large white eggs will cost $3.20 and fifty small white eggs will cost $1.35. I will pay _____ for all of the eggs. If I round this off to the nearest dollar I will need $_____.

(3) Milkmaid: The brown eggs will produce 35 chickens. The large white eggs will produce 80 chickens and the small white eggs will produce 30 chickens. I will then have _____ chickens.

(4) Narrator: The milkmaid walked past six cows, four goats, sixteen pigs, and the farmer's dog. She walked past _____ animals but she did not notice them for she was busy thinking.

(5) Milkmaid: I can sell the chickens from the brown eggs for $25.00. I can sell the chickens from the large white eggs for $75.00 and I will sell the chickens from the small white eggs for $15.00. I will be rich with a total of $_____.

The Milkmaid and Her Pail

Work Space

(6) Milkmaid: I will have enough money from my share to buy a new gown for $30.00, new slippers for $10.00 and new gloves for $5.00. My new outfit will cost $_____. In these fine clothes I will go to the Christmas parties, where all the young fellows will propose to me, but I will toss my head and refuse them every one.

Narrator: At this moment she tossed her head. Down fell the milk pail to the ground, and all her dreams came to an end.

All: Don't count your chickens before they are hatched!

The Milkmaid and Her Pail
Answers are on page 114

Subtraction

The Man, the Boy and the Donkey

Reading Parts: Narrator, Passerby, Man

Work Space

(1) Narrator: A man and his son were going with their donkey to market. They were tired, having walked sixteen miles. The market was 27 miles from their home so they had another _____ miles to walk. They came upon a passerby who said:

(2) Passerby: You fools. A donkey is to ride on. The donkey weighs 300 pounds. You and your boy together weigh 197 pounds. The donkey weighs _____ more pounds than the two of you. It can easily carry you.

(3) Narrator: When they reached the market a woman called out, 'Aren't you ashamed of yourselves for overloading that poor donkey! I know you paid $132.45 for the donkey. I will buy him for $164.00. That will give you a profit of $_____.'

(4) Man: The donkey is not for sale. We will cut down a pole and tie his feet to it and carry him home. That should please everyone. This pole is sixty-seven inches long. We need a five foot pole. We will have to cut off _____ inches.

Narrator: But when the man and the boy walked through the market carrying the donkey, everyone laughed at them.

All: If you try to please everyone, you will please no one.

The Man, the Boy and the Donkey
Answers are on page 114

Subtraction

The Lion and the Mouse

Reading Parts: Narrator, Mouse, Lion

Work Space

(1) Narrator: It was a wild and windy "tickle the nose" day when little mouse went out for a walk. Yesterday she walked 244 feet away from her nest. Today she would walk 333 feet away from her nest. She would walk _____ more feet today than yesterday.

(2) Mouse: It looks like it might rain. I am glad I brought my umbrella. It cost four dollars. I gave the store clerk a twenty dollar bill. I got _____ in change.

(3) Lion: I see a small meal coming my way. I will catch that mouse in my paw and eat her even though I am on a diet. Last month I weighed 522 pounds. This month I weigh 486 pounds. I have lost _____ pounds. One small mouse won't make me gain weight.

(4) Narrator: The lion reached out and caught mouse in his paw. Mouse looked at lion's sharp teeth. Some were missing. A lion should have 32 teeth. Mouse counted 26 teeth. _____ teeth were missing.

(5) Mouse: Please, Sir Lion, if you let me go, perhaps some day I can help you. I am a good seed gatherer. Yesterday I gathered 25 seeds. Today I have gathered 76 seeds. That is _____ more than yesterday.

(6) Lion: I do not eat seeds. I eat mice. But since you are so brave, I will let you go. I am on a diet anyway. Two months from now I hope to weigh 430 pounds I will have lost a total of _____ pounds.

CLC0345 Pieces of Learning © 2005 Polette, Ebbesmeyer

The Lion and the Mouse

(7) Narrator: The lion let the mouse go. Meanwhile some hunters were near. They had $500.00 for hunting supplies. They had paid $120.00 for a big net. They had $_____ left to spend for other supplies. The hunters saw the lion and threw the net over him. Then they went to get their truck to take him to the zoo.

(8) Mouse: Look, the lion is caught in a net. We must help him. Come, mouse friends. 36 of you start chewing at the top of the net. 116 of us will chew at the bottom of the net because it is larger. There will be _____ more mice at the bottom of the net than the top.

Narrator: Mouse and her friends chewed a hole in the net large enough for lion to escape, which just goes to show that:

All: Little friends can be as helpful as big friends.

Work Space

The Lion and the Mouse
Answers are on page 114

Addition
Subtraction

Belling the Cat

Reading Parts: Cat, Mouse Mayor, Mr. Whiskers, Merry Mouse, Narrator

Work Space

(1) Cat: My favorite dinner is a fat juicy mouse. This week I am going to catch and eat 15 more than the 30 I caught and ate last week. This week I will catch and eat _____ mice.

(2) Mouse Mayor: That terrible cat is our enemy. She is eating more and more of us every day. We must call a meeting to see what can be done. There are 228 cellar mice, 120 barn mice and 113 house mice. We must tell them all about the meeting. We must tell _____ mice.

(3) Mr. Whiskers: Mr. Mayor, you have forgotten that the cat caught and ate 30 mice last week. That means there are _____ mice left to tell about the meeting.

(4) Mouse Mayor: No matter. Send the messengers out at once. The meeting will take place in the North Field at midnight. It is 3:00 p.m. now so we have _____hours to tell everyone about the meeting.

(5) Narrator: Merry Mouse was the fastest runner. It took her 66 minutes to tell the cellar mice and 52 minutes to tell the barn mice. Then she rested twenty minutes. After that it took her 44 minutes to tell all of the house mice. Merry Mouse was tired. She had run a total of _____ minutes.

Belling the Cat

(6) Mr. Whiskers: It is time for the meeting. There should be 228 cellar mice here but I count only 203. There are _____ cellar mice missing.

(7) Mouse Mayor: I count 96 barn mice. There should be 120 barn mice here. _____ barn mice are missing. Do you suppose the cat has eaten them?

(8) Merry Mouse: All of the house mice are here. That means there are _____ mice at this meeting. Now we must decide what to do about the cat.

(9) Mr. Whiskers: We could all move to another place. The distance from this farm to the MacGregor farm to the Pickett farm is 38 miles. If the distance from this farm to the MacGregor farm is 22 miles we would need to travel _____ miles more to get to the Pickett farm.

(10) Mouse Mayor: I have an idea. We can draw a triangle on the cellar floor and put up a sign that says NO CATS ALLOWED. One side of the triangle will be 27 feet. One side will be 32 feet. The perimeter of the triangle is 100 feet. That means the third side will be _____ feet. Then we can all stay inside the triangle and be safe.

Merry Mouse: Cats can't read. This cat is sly and quiet. If we could hear the cat coming we can run and hide. I think we should find a big bell and tie it by a ribbon to the cat's neck.

Work Space

Belling the Cat

Narrator: Everyone cheered until Mr. Whiskers got up and said:

Mr. Whiskers: That is all very well, but who is to bell the cat?

All: It is easy to propose impossible solutions.

Belling the Cat
Answers are on page 114

Work Space

Multiplication
Measurement

The Hare and the Tortoise

Reading Parts: Fox, Hare, Tortoise, Narrator

Work Space

(1) Fox: Look at that pokey old tortoise. It takes him two minutes to travel one foot. It will take him _____ minutes to travel three yards.

(2) Tortoise: I am not always slow. I could win a race with Hare if I wanted to. Just the other day I went twice as fast as usual. I traveled one foot in one minute so I traveled three yards in _____ minutes.

(3) Fox: Beat Hare in a race? Nobody can beat Hare in a race. He ran from here to the MacGregor farm in 27 minutes. That means he could make it from here to the farm and back in (less than/more than) an hour.

(4) Narrator: Hare heard what tortoise said and decided to challenge Tortoise to a race. They would run three laps around the farmer's field that had a perimeter of 68 yards. They would run a total of _____ yards.

(5) Fox: Get Ready, Get set, GO! Look at hare run. He is running twenty-two yards a minute. In three minutes he (will/will not) go around the perimeter once time.

Tortoise: Look at Fox go! I think I did too much talking. Now I will just have to keep on walking.

© 2005 Polette, Ebbesmeyer   19   CLC0345 Pieces of Learning

The Hare and the Tortoise

(6) Hare: Here comes the poor Tortoise around the bend. I will hop into that nearby strawberry patch and have strawberries for breakfast. Let's see, there are fifteen rows of strawberries and about 314 strawberries in each row. If I eat them all I can have _____ strawberries for breakfast.

(7) Tortoise: Look at Fox eating those strawberries. And look at all this trash people have scattered around. When the race is over I will go home and get trash bags. Each bag will hold 16 pounds of litter. If I fill seven bags I will have picked up _____ pounds of litter. That will be a very good thing to do.

(8) Fox: There goes Tortoise past the strawberry patch. But I like eating these strawberries. I can gobble down sixteen strawberries in a minute so in 30 minutes I can eat _____ strawberries. Then I will finish the race.

Narrator: Tortoise plodded on and on. When Fox finished eating the strawberries he saw Tortoise near the finish line. He could not run fast enough to cross the finish line before Tortoise. So Fox learned that:

All: Slow and steady wins the race.

Work Space

The Hare and the Tortoise
Answers are on page 114

Multiplication

The Fox and the Goat

Reading Parts: Narrator, Fox, Goat

Work Space

(1) Narrator: Fox spied a small rabbit eating heads of lettuce in the farmer's garden. There were 13 rows with 8 heads of lettuce in each row. Rabbit could choose from a total of _____ heads of lettuce for her meal.

(2) Fox: What a juicy meal rabbit will be. Oh, Oh, she sees me. She is running away. She has already crossed eight fields that are each 46 feet across. She has traveled _____ feet. I must hurry to catch her.

(3) Narrator: Fox was so busy chasing the rabbit that he slipped on a wet stone and fell into a deep well. Having nothing better to do, Fox counted the bricks on one side of the well. There were 80 bricks from top to bottom and 25 bricks from side to side. Since the well had four sides, there was a total of _____ bricks.

(4) Fox: Who is that looking into the well? It is Goat. Come in, Sir Goat. The water is deliciously cool. That's it. Jump right in. Someone has dumped 32 gallons of water in this well each week for fifteen weeks. The well holds at least _____ gallons of water.

Goat: The sides are slippery. How will we get out?

Fox: Let me climb up your horns and then I will pull you out.

The Fox and the Goat

Goat: Good idea!

Narrator: So the fox climbed out and ran away.

All: It is always wise to think before you act.

The Fox and the Goat
Answers are on page 114

Addition
Subtraction
Multiplication

The Grasshopper and the Ants

Reading Parts: Narrator One, Narrator Two, Grasshopper, Ant

Work Space

(1) Narrator One: On a sunny summer day 3 worker ants each carried their food to a spot outside to dry in the sun. Each carried three seeds at a time and each made fourteen trips. They put _____ seeds out to dry.

(2) Narrator Two: The ants were very hard workers. Each round trip to and from their nest under a big log took six minutes. After making fourteen trips the ants had worked a total of _____ minutes. A bright green grasshopper came by and looked at all the food.

(3) Grasshopper: Boy, Oh boy! What a hot day this is! The sun came up at six o'clock this morning and won't set until nine o'clock tonight! That means the ants will work twelve hours every day or _____ hours in a week. Hey, ants, it's too hot to work. Come sing and dance and play with me.

(4) Ant: It may be hot today, the first of August, but winter is coming. The first cold winds will begin to blow on Halloween. That is only _____ days. We must have our food stored by then.

(5) Narrator One: Sure enough the days of summer passed. Cold winds blew. Grasshopper was hungry. He saw a sign that said 'Pizza Parlor.' Another sign said '45 cents each slice.' A whole pizza had eight slices. It would cost grasshopper _____ for two whole pizzas. Grasshopper hopped on. He did not have any money.

© 2005 Polette, Ebbesmeyer   23   CLC0345 Pieces of Learning

The Grasshopper and the Ants

(6) Narrator Two: Grasshopper felt something cold on his back. It was a snowflake. The snow was covering the ground about 3 inches every thirty minutes. In eight hours there would be _____ inches of snow on the ground! Grasshopper hopped over to the ants' nest under the big log.

(7) Grasshopper: Couldn't you spare just a bit of food for me? I have no food at home and I will starve. I only need 20 seeds a day for about 180 days. That is only _____ seeds.

(8) Ant: What did you do last summer? That is the time to gather and store food for winter. Since we stored 33 baskets of seeds, each containing 998 seeds, we have _____ seeds to eat this winter.

Grasshopper: I sang and I danced and I played. It was a merry summer indeed.

Ant: Well, then, you must live this winter on your singing and dancing since that is what you stored up in the summer. Since we spent the summer storing food, that is what we will live on and we did not store enough to share.

All: He who does not prepare for the future must suffer the consequences.

The Grasshopper and the Ants
Answers are on page 114

Work Space

Division

The Boy Who Cried Wolf

Reading Parts: Narrator, Shepherd Boy, Farmer

Work Space

(1) Narrator: There was once a shepherd boy who watched a flock of sheep. There were 120 sheep placed in equal numbers in three pastures. Each pasture held _____ sheep.

(2) Shepherd Boy: I am tired of going from one pasture to another to look after all these sheep. I will be glad when the farmer sells the sheep. He says he will receive $201.00 for three sheep. That means that each sheep will be worth $_____.

(3) Narrator: From six in the morning until six in the evening the shepherd boy went from one pasture to another looking after the sheep. He spent an equal amount of time in each pasture so in one day he spent _____ hours in each pasture. The job was so boring that he often daydreamed.

(4) Shepherd Boy: I will divide the $111.00 I get for the summer's work into three equal parts. One part I will spend. One part I will save and one part I will give to my poor old mother, I will give her $_____.

(5) Farmer: When it is time to shear the sheep there should be enough wool to fill six equal bales with a total weight of 2,040 pounds. That means each bale will weigh_____ pounds. That is a lot of wool!

The Boy Who Cried Wolf

(6) Shepherd Boy: This job is so boring. I would like a little excitement. I will run to the village shouting 'WOLF! WOLF!' and 48 villagers from 12 houses will come running. That would be an average of _____ from each house.

(7) Narrator: The shepherd boy cried 'WOLF! WOLF!' and when the people came to help him he laughed at them. To make matters worse it began to rain. It rained 28 inches in seven minutes. That was _____ inches of rain each minute! The people got very wet. The people got very angry.

(8) Shepherd Boy: The people have all gone back to their homes. That was a great joke to play. But look! What is that coming out of the forest? It is a wolf. I must have help. 'WOLF! WOLF!' Everyone come and help. In 32 minutes the wolf can gobble down eight sheep. He will eat one sheep every_____ minutes. HELP! HELP!

Narrator: No one paid any heed to his cries. No one came to help. The wolf, having no cause to fear, destroyed the whole flock.

All: There is no believing a liar, even when he speaks the truth.

Work Space

The Boy Who Cried Wolf
Answers are on page 114

Division

The Town Mouse and the Country Mouse

Reading Parts: Narrator, Town Mouse, Country Mouse

Work Space

(1) Narrator: A country mouse liked to have visitors. He had at least 144 visitors each year. That was an average of _____ visitors each month. His cousin, a town mouse had never visited. Country mouse called him on the telephone.

(2) Country Mouse: Hello, Town Mouse. I would like you to come and visit. The fall foliage is beautiful. I just purchased a board 192 inches long. I can get _____ 16-inch pieces out of it, just enough for the new room I am putting on my house. You must come and see it.

(3) Town Mouse: I would like very much to visit just as soon as I finish my tail painting class. I don't dare miss a class or I will lose my place. There are only eight classes held each year for a total of 216 mice. That means there is an average of _____ in a class. And there is a long waiting list.

(4) Narrator: Town Mouse finished his tail painting class and came to visit. He did not like the country. He kept calling his friends back in the city. In one week he made sixteen telephone calls for a total of $12.80. That was _____ cents for each call.

© 2005 Polette, Ebbesmeyer   27   CLC0345 Pieces of Learning

The Town Mouse and the Country Mouse

Work Space

(5) Town Mouse: Now that I have visited you, you must come with me. Instead of living with owls and ants, you will have the best of everything. I have spent $312.00 in the last six months for CDs. I spent an equal amount each month so that was $_____ a month I spent to have music in my mouse hole.

(6) Narrator: Country Mouse went to the city with Town Mouse. He had bread, beans, honey, raisins and cheese to eat. Town Mouse explained that he had to make one trip for each eight raisins and he had gathered 128 raisins which meant _____ trips to the kitchen where they were kept. Country Mouse was just about to take a bite when he heard a loud 'MEOW!'

(7) Town Mouse: Stop eating and run! It is the cat! Quick, into that hole It cost $200.00 to have it made just for me. I paid $25.00 down and must pay the rest in seven equal payments of $_____ each. It is good to have a safe place to hide.

Country Mouse: I would rather live outdoors with the ants than in a dark hole. At least I can finish a meal without running from a cat. I am going home.

All: It is better to be safe than to be sorry.

The Town Mouse and the Country Mouse
Answers are on page 115

*Multiplication
Division*

A Wolf in Sheep's Clothing

Reading Parts: Narrator One, Narrator Two, Farmer, Farmer's Wife, Wolf

Work Space

Narrator One:
There was once a sheep farmer who was feeling very pleased with himself.

(1) Farmer: By the time summer comes I will be very rich indeed. The average weight of one of my sheep is 230 pounds and will bring $115.00. That is _____ cents per pound. If each of my fifty sheep is worth $115.00 I will receive $_____ .

(2) Farmer's Wife: Yes, dear, and we will still have the seventy-five Merino sheep whose wool we can sell. The wool from each sheep should be worth at least twenty dollars. That is a total of $_____ we will receive from the wool.

(3) Farmer: And from what we both receive we will have $_____ .

Narrator One: The farmer and his wife were so busy adding up the money they would receive that they did not bother to look after the sheep that night. Just before dawn the next morning a wolf bounded up over a hill and came upon the flock of sheep.

(4) Wolf: Wow! Dinner on the hoof! And am I hungry! There are 50 sheep in the pasture. If I eat two each day, I will have enough food for _____ days. But first I had better disguise myself so the farmer won't know I am here.

© 2005 Polette, Ebbesmeyer   29   CLC0345 Pieces of Learning

A Wolf in Sheep's Clothing

Work Space

Narrator Two: The wolf rolled and rolled on the ground until he was covered with white fluffy wool that had dropped from the backs of the sheep. Now that he looked like a sheep, he could kill and eat one whenever he pleased. The wolf grew fat and lazy for he did not have to work for his dinner.

(5) Wolf: What a life! What a life! But I do seem to be gaining some weight. I weigh 75 pounds now. If I gain 2 pounds a day, in one year I will be the world's largest wolf, weighing _____ pounds!

(6) Narrator One: The next morning just as the sun came up the farmer was busy putting 125 apples in each apple barrel. He had 750 apples so he was not finished until he had filled _____ barrels.

(7) Farmer's Wife: I think we deserve a treat. I made seven trips to the strawberry patch and picked 350 quarts of strawberries. I picked _____ quarts each trip. I will make a strawberry pie for dinner.

Farmer: I will kill one of the sheep so that we can have lamb chops for dinner, too. It will be a fine meal indeed.

(8) Narrator Two: The farmer went to the sheep pasture. He looked and looked again! 16 of his sheep were missing. There were only _____ sheep in the pasture.

CLC0345 Pieces of Learning © 2005 Polette, Ebbesmeyer

A Wolf in Sheep's Clothing

Narrator One: When the sheep saw the farmer coming they ran. Since the wolf in sheep's clothing was so fat, he could not run as fast as the others.

(9) Narrator Two: Thus the farmer caught him first, killed him and the wife cooked him up for dinner. Cooking four lamb chops at fifteen minutes per chop would take _____ hour(s.) When the chops were done the two sat down to eat.

Farmer's Wife: This lamb chop has a very strange taste.

Farmer: It is just your imagination. These are the best lamb chops I have ever tasted!

All: He who fools people may get fooled himself.

A Wolf in Sheep's Clothing
Answers are on page 115

Work Space

Addition
Subtraction
Multiplication
Division

Cinderella

Reading Parts: Cinderella, Isabelle, Odora, Stepmother, Godmother, Prince

Work Space

(1) Cinderella: My name is Cinderella and I have two stepsisters. Isabelle is twenty-six and Odora is twenty-seven. If you add their ages, is the total odd or even? It must be _____.

(2) Odora: I just had to have a new dress for the prince's ball. I needed twelve yards of material. It cost $4.32 a yard so I had to pay _____ plus tax.

(3) Isabelle: I wanted new dancing slippers. The cheapest pair cost $16.75. The pair I want costs $32.00. I will have to pay _____ more than the cheapest pair.

(4) Cinderella: I have to scrub every brick on the fireplace every day. The fireplace has 100 bricks on each side and fifty bricks at the top. That means I scrub _____ bricks every week!

(5) Isabelle: I spent eight hours a day for three days getting ready for the ball. Odora spent six hours a day for five days getting ready for the ball. Odora spent ____ more hours than I did getting ready. But then, she is not as pretty as I am. She needs more time.

(6) Cinderella: I was told to go and buy a new broom to sweep the cottage. The regular price of the broom was $4.50 but I got it on sale for half price so the broom only cost _____.

Cinderella

Work Space

(7) Odora: At last the night of the ball has arrived. Mother hired a coach to take us to the ball at $6.00 an hour plus a $5.00 tip. My mother, sister and I plan to be away five hours. She will pay _____ for the coach.

(8) Cinderella: At last they are gone. But look at the work I have to do. Washing dishes will take 20 minutes. Scrubbing floors will take 60 minutes. Ironing clothes will take 120 minutes. Scrubbing the fireplace bricks will take another 120 minutes and darning their nightgowns will take another 40 minutes. Why, that is _____ hours of work! Wait! What is that noise?

(9) Fairy Godmother: Hello, my dear. I am sorry it took me so long to get here. I had two hundred miles to travel and the coach could only go twenty miles a day. I have been traveling _____ days. One sweep of my wand and your work is all done. Now we must get you ready for the ball.

(10) Cinderella: Oh, what a beautiful dress, and glass slippers, too, and a 125 carat diamond necklace. Since each carat costs two hundred dollars, this necklace is worth _____. I can't possibly wear something this expensive.

(11) Fairy Godmother: You deserve the best, my dear. Now into the coach you go. Remember, you must be home by midnight and it is seven p.m. now so you have _____ hours to enjoy yourself.

Cinderella

(12) Cinderella: This is so exciting watching all the dancers. There were 22 dancers for the first dance, 34 dancers for the second dance and 16 dancers for the third dance. That is an average of _____ dancers for each dance.

(13) Prince: Beautiful lady, will you dance the rest of the evening with me? I have asked the orchestra to play 18 ten-minute songs with a ten-minute rest each hour. We will dance _____ hours and rest _____ minutes.

(14) Cinderella: I have danced all evening, but look at the clock. It is almost midnight. I must run. Look at these 540 palace steps. I can run down three steps a second. It will take me _____ minutes to get down all the steps. Oh, dear, I have lost a slipper. But I do not have time to go back and find it.

(15) Prince: This slipper must belong to some girl in the kingdom. I have visited 216 homes with an average of three maidens in each home. That means I have tried this slipper on _____ feet. My knees are getting sore from kneeling down. Here is one last cottage. Let's see what happens here.

(16) Isabella and Odora: The slipper belongs to one of us. We will make it fit. While we are trying it on, won't you have some tea? We made four quarts so you can have all _____ ounces if you like.

Work Space

Cinderella

(17) Prince: It is obvious that the slipper does not fit you. But wait, who is that scrubbing the fireplace? Come and try on the slipper. It fits! I have dreamed of finding you eight hours a night for three weeks. You have been in my dreams a total of _____ hours. Come away with me to the palace.

(18) Stepmother: But you must first pay me for giving Cinderella food and shelter for the past five years since her father died. The charge is five dollars a day so you owe me _____ dollars.

(19) Prince: You can come to the palace and collect your money when a millennium has passed which is _____ years. In the meantime, Cinderella and I plan to live happily ever after.

Work Space

Cinderella
Answers are on page 115

Addition
Subtraction
Multiplication
Division

The Golden Goose

Reading Parts: Narrator, Father, Hans, Old Man, Dummling, Princess, King, Innkeeper

Work Space

(1) Narrator: A man had two sons. The oldest, Hans, liked to brag. The youngest was called Dummling and was made fun of by others. Hans lived in a room that was 20 by 20 feet. Dummling had a closet to sleep in that was three by three feet. Hans had _____ more square feet of space than Dummling.

(2) Father: Hans, go into the woods and cut down six trees. Each tree should take 30 minutes to cut down. You will be gone for _____ hours. Take this cake with you in case you get hungry.

(3) Hans: I have only cut down two trees but I am hungry. I will have the cake. But who is that coming? It is an old gray man. He is 30 yards away but moving six yards a minute. He will be here in _____ minutes. I will eat fast so that I have nothing to share with him.

(4) Old Man: Greetings. Do you have food to spare? I ate yesterday afternoon at two o'clock. It is now six o'clock in the evening. I have not eaten in _____ hours.

(5) Hans: I have no food for you. Besides I have to cut down six trees. My father will sell the wood from each for $36.00. That is a total of $_____. I must get to work. OUCH! The axe has cut my arm. I must go home and have it looked to.

CLC0345 Pieces of Learning　　　36　　　© 2005 Polette, Ebbesmeyer

The Golden Goose

(6) Dummling: Father, let me go and cut the trees down. I know where there are three rows of trees with eight trees in each row. That is _____ trees. I can cut them all down in twelve hours. That is _____ tree(s) an hour.

(7) Father: Very well. Go and cut the trees. Here is a loaf of stale bread. Cook is out of sugar for cake. I gave her $4.25 to buy five pounds of sugar when the market opens. That is $_____ per pound. But the market will not be open before you leave.

(8) Narrator: Dummling went into the forest carrying his axe and his loaf of bread which contained sixteen stale slices, and met the old man. He shared half his bread with the man. Each ate _____ slices.

(9) Old Man: Since you have shared your food with me I will give you a gift. Walk 122 steps east, 143 steps west and 12 steps north or a total of _____ steps. You will find a golden goose waiting for you by an old tree.

(10) Narrator: Sure enough, Dummling found a goose whose feathers were made of gold. Each feather must be worth $1000.00 which was $_____ more than one tree would bring. Dummling was very tired so he stopped at an inn for the night.

(11) Innkeeper: The room is $12.35 for the night. Two towels are sixty-five cents each and supper is $1.35. You will owe a total of $_____.

Work Space

The Golden Goose

Work Space

(12) Narrator: Dummling paid the Innkeeper and went to sleep in his room. The Innkeeper's seven daughters saw the goose. As each tried to pluck a golden feather, her hand stuck tight to the goose. Each girl weighed ninety pounds. The goose weighed four pounds. When Dummling left the next morning he pulled _____ pounds behind him.

(13) Princess: Father, Father, look at the funny sight! A man is followed by seven women stuck to a goose! This is the first time I have laughed in many years. I must marry this man who makes me laugh. I will need 12 yards of lace at $4.32 per yard for my wedding gown. I will need a total of $_____.

(14) King: Daughter, you can only marry this nobody if he can bring me a ship that can sail on land or on water. In my younger days I vowed to sail 5000 miles around the world. I have only sailed 2864 miles. I must finish the trip by sailing another _____ miles.

(15) Narrator: Dummling went to see the old man who gave him a ship that could sail on land or water. He and the Princess were married. Their wedding was attended by 1090 guests. The food and drink cost $5.00 per guest for a total of _____. It was a very expensive wedding.

All: And Dummling and the Princess lived happily ever after.

The Golden Goose Answers are on page 115

Fractions

The Tower of the Dragon

Reading Parts: Narrator One, Narrator Two, Princess, Brother One, Brother Two, Younger Brother, King, Shepherd Boy

Work Space

(1) Narrator One: Once upon a time there was a king who had three sons and a daughter. He kept the daughter in a gold and silver cage and guarded her as carefully as the eyes in his head. 5/8 of the cage was made of gold and _____ of the cage was made of silver.

(2) Princess: Please, father, won't you allow me to go out and take a walk around the castle with my brothers? The distance on each side of the castle is 82 1/2 feet and at each end is 34 1/2 feet. That means I can walk a distance of _____ feet. And I really need the exercise! The father consented.

(3) Narrator One: Hardly was she out the door when a dragon came swooping down out of the sky. His flying speed was 90 1/2 miles an hour that meant he could fly _____ miles in two hours. This terrible dragon seized the maiden and carried her away deep into the forest before her brothers could as much as offer a shout in her defense.

(4) Brother One: Father! Father! A terrible dragon has captured our sister. Please give us permission to go and rescue her. We will each need money for the trip. We need $80.00 for horses, $25.00 for bows and arrows, $5.00 for a rope and $15.00 for an axe. We have 1/2 of the money we need. Will you give us $_____?

(5) King: Very well, here is the money for the bow and

© 2005 Polette, Ebbesmeyer   39   CLC0345 Pieces of Learning

The Tower of the Dragon

arrow, rope, and axe. But I cannot afford to buy the horses. Even at 1/4 off, the horses would cost $ _____ .

(6) Brother Two: The trip to the dragon's lair will take four hours on foot but only 1 1/2 hours on horseback. We will save _____ hours travel time if we have horses.

(7) Narrator One: The king consented and after many wanderings the brothers came upon a tower which stood neither upon earth or in heaven. This was indeed the place where their sister was held captive. There was no door at the foot of the tower. At the top, three hundred feet into the sky, only one small window could be seen. Each brother's rope was 55 3/4 feet long. That was a total of _____ feet, not enough to reach the top of the tower.

(8) Brother Two: We must make a plan to reach the top of the tower. Youngest brother is a good climber. See that tall tree! It reaches to the top of the tower. He can climb up and then jump into the window. If he climbs 20 feet a minute he will only take _____ minutes to climb to the top.

(9) Youngest Brother: Wow! That was a hard climb. Look at the two doors in this room. Which one shall I open? The one on the right is two feet by five feet. The one on the left is 32 1/2 inches by 61 1/2 inches. I will open the smallest door. It is the one on the _____ .

(10) Princess: Oh, youngest brother, you must flee before the dragon awakes. He said he would sleep six

Work Space

The Tower of the Dragon

hours and he has already been sleep 1/3 of that time. He will awaken in _____ minutes.

(11) Younger Brother: I will deal the dragon a heavy blow on the head. Take that and that and that! But look, he does not awaken! I will give him 25 blows every half minute for five minutes for a total of _____ blows. That should awaken him.

(12) Princess: Blows won't kill the Dragon. Come, let us escape! But first you must meet the other maidens the Dragon has captured and imprisoned. He stole each away from her family because of her beauty and her very special treasure. This is Mattie. She was stolen from a farm along with her spinning wheel which spins straw into gold. She can spin 210 gold pieces in 3/4 of an hour. That is _____ gold pieces every eight hours!

(13) Younger Brother: And who is this lovely girl stringing pearls? At her feet is a golden hen picking up pearls from a golden box 2 3/4 feet wide and 3 feet long. Each square foot of space in the box holds 2,000 pearls. That is a total of _____ pearls. I see her name written on the box, Isabelle!

(14) Narrator One: The Princess and her brother then went back into the room where the Dragon lay, dragged him out, and threw him head-foremost down to the earth. Since he fell at a rate of 7/8 foot per second it took _____ seconds to complete the fall.

(15) Brother One: Look, the dragon is dead! And

Work Space

The Tower of the Dragon

Work Space

Younger Brother is helping our sister and two other maidens to reach the tree by the tower window. They are climbing down. Our horses can carry only 325 pounds. I weigh 180 pounds. You weigh 201 pounds and each fair lady weighs about 100 pounds. Each of us (can or cannot) carry a lady on our horse.

(16) Brother Two: We do not want to go back to our father and tell him that youngest brother is the hero. We must chop the tree down and leave him in the tower so that he has no means of escape. It will take 1800 blows of the axe to chop the tree down. At 10 blows each minute, it will take us _____ hours. We had better get started.

Narrator Two: Even though their sister, the Princess, protested, they warned her they would return and kill Younger Brother if she breathed a word of their scheme to their father or anyone else. Thus, she and the other maidens held their silence. Then they rode away, taking younger brother's horse with them. On their way back to the castle they came upon a shepherd boy.

(17) Shepherd boy: Sheep for sale! Sheep for sale. Each costs $36.00. Buy four at 1/4 off. Each will then cost only $_____, or _____ for four.

(18) Brother One: We don't want to buy four sheep but

The Tower of the Dragon

we will give you a home in a castle if you will come with us. Here, put these clothes on. They belonged to our younger brother who is no longer with us. He departed this world the first of January, and it is now the first of May. Thus he has been gone _____ days. You will take his place.

(19) Narrator Two: The days passed. Meanwhile back at the tower, Younger Brother had not slept for three and 3/4 days as he pondered a way to escape. He had been thinking and thinking for a total of _____ hours.

(20) Younger Brother: I must escape! I know what to do. I will make a rope of pearls and climb down the 300 foot tower. If each half foot of rope takes 24 pearls I will need _____ pearls to make a rope that is long enough.

(21) Narrator Two: On the day of the wedding, Younger Brother appeared in the midst of the 100 wedding guests as they were entering the church. The door to the church was only five feet tall. 3/4 of the wedding guests were shorter than five feet. That meant that _____ guests would have to stoop down to enter the church.

(22) Princess: Your brothers threatened to kill you if we told how they left you in the tower. Listen everyone, here is the true hero. His brothers had planned to hide him away for at least a decade which is _____ years.

(23) Narrator Two: In a trice the Prince was greeted by

Work Space

The Tower of the Dragon

Work Space

the wedding guests, but his eyes sought out the beautiful Mattie. When he found her, he took her hand and asked her to be his bride. He would build a castle for her that cost 2/3 more than his father's $160,000 castle. The new castle would cost $ _____.

(24) Narrator One: The young Prince (who was only twenty-one) and Mattie were married and the Prince was made heir to the throne. He was to rule until his death at the age of 89 and 1/2, a total of _____ years.

The Tower of the Dragon
Answers are on page 115

Fractions

Hansel and Gretel

Reading Parts: Narrator, Stepmother, Father, Hansel, Gretel, Witch

Work Space

(1) Narrator: In a great forest lived a poor woodcutter, his wife, and two children called Hansel and Gretel. The woodcutter had traveled 6 and ¾ miles to town and back again for a total of _____ miles. But he brought home no food for he could not sell his wood.

(2) Stepmother: I have only 1/4 cup of oatmeal. You have 3/4 of a cup of oatmeal. If we put them together and share equally we would each have only _____ cup of oatmeal to eat and there is nothing for the children.

(3) Father: Look at all the wood I have cut. I stacked 2/7 of it yesterday and 3/7 of it today. I still have _____ of the wood to stack. But I don't know why I bother. No one will buy it.

(4) Stepmother: We will starve to death unless we get rid of the children. Tomorrow we will take them into the forest. We will walk 40 ½ feet to the north and 82 3/4 feet to the west for a total of _____ feet. There the path ends and we will take them deep into the forest and leave them there with a crust of bread.

Narrator: The man would rather starve than give up his children, but having nothing to feed them, thought they might survive on berries and fruits they would find in the woods.

© 2005 Polette, Ebbesmeyer   45   CLC0345 Pieces of Learning

Hansel and Gretel

Work Space

(5) Narrator: Now Hansel overheard the woman's plans so before leaving the next morning he put a slice of bread in his pocket. As they walked along he broke off bread crumbs and left them on the path. He could get 9 crumbs from each 1/4 of the bread slice or a total of ____ crumbs. The children were led deeper and deeper into the forest.

(6) Stepmother: See, children, I am making you a fire. When you are tired you can sleep a little. We are going into the forest to cut wood. With my help your father can cut 2 1/2 cords in three hours. When six hours have passed and he has cut _____ cords, we will come and fetch you.

(7) Hansel: Wake up, Gretel. The fire burned 3 1/4 hours. I added wood so it burned another 3 1/4 hours. That is a total of _____ hours the fire has burned. No one has come for us. But when the moon comes out we can follow the bread crumbs that I dropped and will soon be home.

(8) Narrator: Sad to say, the children could not follow the crumbs for the birds had eaten them. Then it began to rain. 1 and 1/16 inches fell in the first hour and 4 and 5/16 inches fell the rest of the night for a total of _____ inches of rain. The children were cold, wet and hungry when they reached a little house.

(9) Gretel: Look! The house is built of loaves of bread. Each side contains 14 and 1/2 loaves and there are four equal sides. That is _____ loaves of bread.

CLC0345 Pieces of Learning   46   © 2005 Polette, Ebbesmeyer

Hansel and Gretel

Work Space

(10) Hansel: The windows are pure sugar and the roof is made of 10 yards of candy canes. If I eat 3 and 1/4 yards of candy canes now, there will be _____ yards of candy canes left for tomorrow.

(11) Gretel: Look at the marshmallow steps! One step is 8 7/8 inches, one step is 6 1/4 inches and the top step is 7 1/2 inches. That is a total of _____ inches of marshmallows we can eat.

(12) Hansel: Look! This bag says it has 1 1/2 pounds of carmels and here is another with 2 5/8 pounds of carmels. That is _____ pounds of carmels. Wait! What is that sound?

(13) Witch: Nibble, nibble, gnaw. Who is nibbling at my little house. 1/4 of my bread loaves have fallen to the ground. That is _____ loaves. Oh, I see two hungry children. Come in, your poor children. No harm shall come to you. (See #9)

(14) Narrator: On the table the children saw pancakes with sugar, apples and nuts. There were three quarts of milk, each 2/3 full or a total of _____ quarts. The hungry children sat down and ate.

Hansel and Gretel

Work Space

(15) Witch: (softly) I cannot see far with my red eyes, but I smelled the children coming near. I have them now, and they shall not escape. While the girl is sleeping, I will grab the boy and lock him in the stable. To tie him up I need ropes of different lengths: 8 5/8 inches, 10 1/2 inches, 7 3/16 inches, and 9 inches. I will need a total of _____ inches of rope.

(16) Narrator: While the children slept, the witch put Hansel in the stable and shook Gretel awake. She gave Gretel a pail that holds eight quarts of water. Gretel was to fill the 24 quart caludron which was only 2/3 full. She would need to add _____ more quarts to fill the cauldron.

(17) Witch: Now, I have lit the fire in my special oven which takes 3 3/4 hours to heat properly. Go quickly and get more wood. If I add twice as much wood the oven will heat in 1/3 of the time or _____ hours.

(18) Gretel: (Softly) I know the old woman means to harm us. She says she is baking 36 cupcakes and that 2/3 of them or _____ cupcakes will be chocolate. Perhaps it is more than cupcakes she means to bake. She is pointing at me. She wants me to put my head in the oven to see if it is warm enough. I will ask her to show me how.

(19) Witch: Silly goose. The door is 36 1/4 inches by 28 1/2 inches. That is _____ square inches, big enough even for me to fit in. Here, I will show you.

CLC0345 Pieces of Learning 48 © 2005 Polette, Ebbesmeyer

Hansel and Gretel

(20) Narrator: As soon as the witch had climbed in the oven, Gretel shut the door and fastened the bolt. She ran like lightning to the stable, untied Hansel, and set him free. They went into the witch's house and in each of four corners stood a chest of jewels weighing 20 and 1/2 pounds. There was a total of _____ pounds of jewels!

(21) Hansel: We must take what we can carry back to father so we will never be poor again. Come, we have a long walk ahead of us. If we walk 2 1/2 miles each hour, we will have walked _____ miles in six hours.

(22) Narrator: The trip home was 12 5/9 miles. The children could only walk 7 1/9 miles before dark. They slept on the soft ferns of the forest floor and the next morning they walked the remaining _____ miles home.

(23) Father: Oh, children, how I have missed you. Your stepmother left when I told her I was going to search for you. You will not starve. The Mayor has asked me to use the wood I have cut to build 17 houses on 8 1/2 acres of land. Each house will be built on _____ acre(s).

Narrator: So the jewels were not needed after all, and Hansel and Gretel and their father lived happily ever after.

Hansel and Gretel
Answers are on page 116

Work Space

Decimals
Percents

The Fisherman and His Wife

Reading Parts: Narrator, Fisherman, Wife, Fish

Work Space

(1) Narrator: There was once a fisherman who lived with his wife in a pig sty near a big lake. Every day he went out fishing. On Monday he caught 8.7 pounds of fish, on Tuesday 12.4 pounds, on Wednesday 3.6 pounds, and on Thursday 13.7 pounds. So far during the week he had caught a total of _____ pounds of fish.

(2) Fisherman: It has been a good week for catching fish. My wife and I will not go hungry even if we do live in a pig sty. So far today I have caught a six-pound bass and an eight-pound bass. The eight-pound fish is _____ percent larger than the six-pound fish. But here comes the largest fish of all. What a treat it will be for dinner!

(3) Fish: Fisherman, I ask you to let me live, for I am no fish but an enchanted prince. Put me in the water again, and I will grant you whatever you wish. Perhaps you would like an income of $25.75 per week. That would be a total of $_____ each year, far more than you can earn catching fish.

(4) Fisherman: I must ask my wife what she wishes for, and then I will return. It will take a long time to go all around the lake to get home. It is 143.87 yards on one side and 131.9 yards on the other. To go all the way around, I would have to walk _____ yards.

Narrator: The fisherman returned home and told his wife about their good fortune. She was not at all pleased.

The Fisherman and His Wife

Work Space

(5) Wife: Why would you take just a few dollars from the fish when it will grant any wish? How hard it is to live in a pig sty which stinks and is so disgusting. Tell the fish we want a castle with 373 rooms and 450 servants. That would be _____ servants for each room.

(6) Fisherman: I can't go now. It is starting to rain. We have had an average of .641 inches a month for the last six months. That means _____ inches of rain have fallen in the last 6 months.

(7) Wife: Never mind the rain. Go and tell the fish what I want. And don't forget to say that I want a great hall paved with 5280 tiles and that 60% of the tiles must be made of gold. That will be _____ golden tiles. Here is a list of other things you can ask for as well.

(8) Fisherman: I'm glad I decided to walk back to the lake. Look at the beautiful flowers. If I bought them in the store, daffodils would be $1.89, roses $1.29, violets $.59 and daisies, $.89. I will save $ _____ by picking them here, and my wife will be so pleased. Or at least I think she will. She seems to be getting harder and harder to please these days.

(9) Fish: Hello fisherman. Before you tell me your wife's wish, take this bag of gold coins worth $600.00 and divide it equally among 40 poor people. Each person will receive $_____.

© 2005 Polette, Ebbesmeyer   CLC0345 Pieces of Learning

The Fisherman and His Wife

(10) Fisherman: I will do as you ask, kind fish. My wife wishes to live in a great castle of 373 rooms and a great hall with golden tiles and 450 servants. She also wants a coach and horses that can travel 180.6 miles in 3.8 hours. That is a speed of _____ miles per hour.

Fish: Go to it then, she is standing before the castle door.

(11) Narrator: When the fisherman arrived home he found a great palace, a hall paved with gold and many servants. There was a courtyard 22.6 yards by 11.8 yards or _____ square yards, and stables for the horses and the very best of carriages.

(12) Narrator: Each day the wife went riding in her carriage. The first week she traveled 383.7 miles. The second week she traveled 412.4 miles. The third week she traveled 139.9 miles and the fourth week she traveled 273.8 miles. In one month she had traveled _____ miles. She saw the people of the land hard at work. But none bowed to her as her carriage passed by.

Wife: Husband, go at once to the fish and tell him that living in a castle with golden floors and servants and horses and a beautiful carriage is not enough. I want all the people to bow as I ride by. I want to be queen of all the land!

Fisherman: It will not end well. The land already has a queen. To ask for more is shameful.

Work Space

The Fisherman and His Wife

Narrator: When the fisherman reached the lake it was quite black and began to boil up from below. The angry fish appeared and asked what the wife wanted now.

Fisherman: She wishes to be queen of all the land.

Fish: Go home and find your ungrateful wife back in the pig sty.

All: And that is where they are living to this day.

The Fisherman and His Wife
Answers are on page 116

Putting It All Together

HERMES, THE MERRY OLYMPIAN

Reading Parts: Narrator One, Narrator Two, Hermes (her-mees), Apollo, Zeus, Mother

Work Space

(1) Narrator One: Hermes was the jolliest of the gods on Mount Olympus. He was the god of those who lived by their wits, and that included merchants and thieves. His mother was a daughter of a Titan. The two lived in a deep cave in one of the mountains. Hermes was forever getting in trouble. He was barely walking when he stole out of the cave one dark night and traveled to Apollo's pasture to steal some cows. He knew his mother checked on him every hour. He had left the cave at 2:35 A.M. and it was now 3:18. He had been gone _____ minutes. He would have to hurry!

(2) Hermes: I've lost too much time trying to count how many cows Apollo has. It's a good thing I didn't have to travel far. I'd better take what I want and get back to the cave, since I have only _____ minutes before mother checks on me again. Oh, but this is fun! I love to play tricks on Apollo. He will be furious!

(3) Narrator Two: Hermes quickly gathered 150 of the best cows and took 1/3 of them with him. Hermes was very sly. He tied brooms to the tails of the _____ cows he had taken, so they would erase their own tracks and drove them backwards out of the pasture. He tied branches on his own feet to make them look like giant's tracks and then hurried back to his home in the cave.

HERMES, THE MERRY OLYMPIAN

(4) Hermes: I've got to get these cows into the pen in my secret grove before day breaks. I'm glad I sacrificed 2 of them to the 12 most important Olympians. If they divide each of them into 36 equal pieces, each of them will receive _____ pieces. And look at these interesting entrails I took from the cow's insides. I have seven strings of them. After I've strung them over this empty tortoise shell, I believe I'll be able to create beautiful music. I'll call my instrument a lyre. But first, I must get back to the cave before Mother finds me gone.

(5) Mother: Hermes! Don't think you can sneak back here after being gone most of the night! I saw you leave at 2:38 A.M. I waited _____ minutes, until 3:00 A.M., hoping you would return quickly. Now, hours later, it's almost dawn and I'm sure you were out there stealing Apollo's cows. Shame on you!!

(6) Hermes: Please understand, Mother! I did what I had to do for both of us. I am an Olympian, and we should be living in glory on Mount Olympus! It's because of Hera's jealousy that we're stuck in this dark cave. She can't bear the thought of me being Zeus's son. She had better not try to turn Zeus against his sons. He is King and he has 7,836 thunderbolts to use against those who anger him. Does she realize that number of bolts represents 7 x _____ thousand, 8 x_____hundred, 3 x _____ + 6? She had better be careful how she and my brother, Apollo, treat us.

Work Space

HERMES, THE MERRY OLYMPIAN

(7) Narrator One: Just then, Apollo stormed into the cave and jerked Hermes from his bed, demanding that his cows be returned at once. Even though Hermes whimpered and lied about stealing the cows, Apollo turned on him in anger and chased him out of the cave. Hermes offered to pay $45.50 for each cow, but the total of _____ dollars did not interest the wealthy Apollo. He chased Hermes straight to Mount Olympus. When they arrived, all the Olympians laughed to see little Hermes chased by a furious Apollo.

(8) Apollo: Please, Father Zeus, tell this thief to give back my cows at once. He took 50 of my best 500 cows. That's _____ percent of my prize cows. He's a thief and a liar. He told me there were no cows in his cave. But I know that he took them!

(9) Hermes: I am *not* a liar! There is not one cow in the cave. I'm just a poor helpless babe being bullied by the mighty Apollo. He may be my brother, but you are my father. I beg you to help me, great Zeus! I've been told you have 7,836 thunderbolts. If you round that number to the nearest 1000, you have _____ bolts. Could you spare a few to put Apollo in his place?

Work Space

HERMES, THE MERRY OLYMPIAN

Work Space

(10) Zeus: Hermes, you are a sly little trickster. You've given us all a good laugh. But I want you to tell Apollo where the cows are hidden. I want you to be good friends with your brother. To reward you, I'm giving you a golden hat with wings, a pair of winged sandals and a cape to hide your magic tricks. With your wings, you'll be able to cover the 600 miles back to the cave in 1/3 the time of my fastest runner. It would take him 3 hours, but you'll be back in _____ hour. Go now and take Apollo with you.

(11) Narrator Two: Hermes had to obey his father and, with no more tricks, he took his brother to the woods where the cows were hidden. Apollo was so happy to see his cows again, he forgave Hermes. That is, until he counted them and found two missing. Seeing this, Hermes had to think fast. He had 29 ideas in mind, but 13 wouldn't work, 4 took too much time, and _____ would make Zeus angry. That left him with no ideas in mind, but he had his lyre and knew that music could sooth the angry man as well as the angry beast.

(12) Hermes: I can see how angry you are, Apollo. I don't blame you, but before you get any angrier, I want to show you my new musical instrument and play a tune for you. I learned 253 melodies very quickly and added 198 more. Of those I have discarded 62. So I have _____ melodies left to play for you. I hope the sound will bring you pleasant thoughts. Your appreciation of music is known throughout the world.

HERMES, THE MERRY OLYMPIAN

(13) Narrator One: As Hermes began to play, Apollo listened in awe. It was the most beautiful music he had ever heard, and he soon forgot his anger. He begged Hermes to play all of the melodies. Finally, after playing 113 tunes, Hermes stopped. But Apollo talked him into 12 encores before Hermes was too tired to play the last of the _____ tunes he had learned.

(14) Apollo: I must have that instrument, Hermes. I am known all over the earth for my music, and I will give you my entire herd of cows for the lyre. You will be my best friend and I will throw in my magic wand as well. With it you can multiply any 6,000 wishes at least 18 times. Just think! Instead of 6,000 wishes, you'll have _____ wishes come true.

Narrator Two: Hermes agreed to the bargain and Zeus was pleased. He made Hermes the messenger of the Olympians and brought Hermes and his mother to Mount Olympus to live. They lived there in happiness because of Hermes' great popularity. Hermes never lied or stole again. He learned to be liked for his generosity and good works.

HERMES, THE MERRY OLYMPIAN

Answers are on page 116

Work Space

Putting It All Together

THE STORY OF DAPHNE AND APOLLO

Reading Parts: Narrator One, Narrator Two, Apollo, Cupid, Daphne, Father

Work Space

(1) Narrator One: Apollo was the god of light and truth. One day, when he was a young man, he found Cupid, the god of love, playing with his bow and arrows. Apollo was angry for he wanted no one to mix up his arrow collection. He had 48,236,409 silver arrows, 3,815,725 golden arrows and 2,134,524 plain arrows. Apollo knew he had _____ arrows in all. He did *not* want Cupid mixing them up.

(2) Apollo: Cupid! What are you doing with my arrows and bow? I have slain the great serpent with them! I'll have no one touching them but me. I see you haven't touched my silver arrows, but the golden and plain arrows are all mixed up. Not counting the silver ones, you will be separating a total of _____ golden and plain arrows. You had better get busy!

(3) Cupid: Watch who you're ordering about, Apollo. You may destroy serpents, but my arrows are more powerful than yours. I may even decide to wound you with them! I too, have golden arrows; 8,216,343 of them. And I had 5,455,904 blunt-tipped, lead arrows which can destroy all love in your life and I have used only 34,503 of the lead ones. So be careful, for you know I have _____ of these dangerous lead arrows left.

© 2005 Polette, Ebbesmeyer   59   CLC0345 Pieces of Learning

THE STORY OF DAPHNE AND APOLLO

Work Space

(4) Narrator Two: After threatening Apollo, Cupid flew up to the top of the highest mountain. He needed to find out how many lead arrows he had left - that would ruin the thought of love in any person - and how many he had of the golden arrows that made a person instantly fall in love. He found the total of his lead and golden arrows came to _____ .

(5) Cupid: I haven't the time to get an exact count of my two kinds of arrows, so I will just round the numbers. I know that I had 5,455,904 lead arrows. After using 34,503 of them, there will be 5,421,401 arrows left. Since the number to the right of my 5 million is less than 5, I'll just round the number of lead arrows down to 5 million. I know that if the number had been greater than 5, I would have had to round the number up to 6 million. Quickly now I'll round the remaining 8,216,343 gold arrows to the number _____. Good! I have plenty of arrows to use against Apollo.

(6) Narrator One: As Cupid finished sorting and counting his arrows, he looked down into the wooded valley and spied Daphne, a beautiful wood nymph. He knew of Apollo's love for her and decided to get his revenge with his lead arrows. There were 33 wood nymphs dancing around. If he shot five arrows into each of them, he would need _____ arrows.

THE STORY OF DAPHNE AND APOLLO

Work Space

(7) Daphne: I am the goddess of wild things, and I love to run in these deep, dark woods. I love my freedom and the fields where I can roam to my heart's content. I will stay here forever among these beautiful trees. I wonder how many trees there are in my beautiful forest! I will try to figure the number in my head. On this side of the path, there are 47 large trees and 28 small ones. To make it easier, I'll add 47 to 30 to get _____ and subtract 2 to find out there are _____ trees on this side.

(8) Narrator Two: Daphne was enjoying her mental addition and subtraction, but she failed to see the blunt-tipped arrow that Cupid had aimed at her heart. As the arrow flew through the air, it became invisible. When it pierced her heart, she felt a sharp pain, but didn't know why. However, the arrow did its work, and Daphne lost all thoughts of love. She rushed to her father, the river god, who was trying to decide how many boats he would need for his water nymphs. There were 31 nymphs and each boat could hold 7. He decided he would need _____ boats to each hold 7 nymphs with a remainder of _____ in the last boat.

(9) Father: Daphne, what are you doing here and why are you crying so hard? Did someone hurt you? You look exhausted. I know your journey from the woods takes 5 hours and 11 minutes, so you have been traveling for _____ minutes. What is troubling you to make such a long trip?

THE STORY OF DAPHNE AND APOLLO

(10) Daphne: Oh Father, promise me that I will never have to marry. Promise that you will help me escape anyone who wants to marry me. I never want to fall in love or have children. I just want to be free to roam my woods. The gods have given me 7/8 of the woods to explore and claim as my own. I have only explored 4/8 of them. I have _____ left to discover. I will have no time or desire to spend on love!

(11) Father: Very well, Daphne. If this is your wish, I will grant it. However, some gods will be displeased, and I will have to pay them off. Zeus will demand $88.00. Athena will need $57.33, Hera must have $75.32 and Pan will ask for $49.68. In all I will have to pay_____. I will gladly pay the amount to make you happy. Now go in peace to roam your beloved woods.

(12) Narrator One: Cupid watched as Daphne hurried back to the woods. His plans were working out perfectly. That wasn't always the case! He had to figure on the probability of things happening his way. There was always the element of chance! Because Cupid was a god, he had twice the chance of succeeding as the nymphs did and the unexpected. Since Cupid's chances of success were doubled, he knew that Daphne had only 1/4 chance, while he had _____ chances of success. So he drew out a golden arrow and aimed it at Apollo who had just reunited with Daphne in the woods. Apollo instantly fell in love with the nymph.

Work Space

THE STORY OF DAPHNE AND APOLLO

Work Space

(13) Apollo: Oh Daphne! I am the Son of Jupiter. I've slain the great serpent with my arrow. But now I fear that Cupid's arrow has wounded me seriously. You must stay with me for I can never stop pursuing you, no matter how far or how fast you run! I am swifter than you and I can cover 5 miles in 10 minutes. Imagine covering _____ feet in 10 minutes! You could never do it! So stop now!!

(14) Narrator Two: Daphne continued to run, but she realized that she had gone only 1/2 mile in the last 10 minutes and knowing that was only _____ feet, she would soon be caught by Apollo. With her last bit of strength, she called out to her father, the river god.

(15) Daphne: Help me Father! Help me! You promised that you would help me escape anyone who wanted to marry me, and I need you now!! Apollo has pursued me for 15 minutes and covered _____ feet in that time. I have no chance to escape his speed.

(16) Narrator One: No sooner had Daphne uttered this plea to her Father, than her arms and legs turned to wood. Her hair became leaves. From her feet grew roots that went deep into the ground. Some roots were 1 kilometer long, but the longest was 3 times that length at _____ meters. Daphne had turned into a laurel tree and nothing was left of her, but her loveliness.

THE STORY OF DAPHNE AND APOLLO

(17) Apollo: Oh Daphne, what have you done to yourself? I feel that I have lost you forever, but still I know that your heart is beating beneath the bark of this tree. I weep for what I have lost, but I will use your wood for my harp and for my arrows. In that way, you will be with me forever. I'll weave your branches into a wreath for my head. I will take 15 inch-long branches and divide them into 4 equal lengths. Each length will be _____ inches long - just long enough for weaving. That way, I will carry you with me for all time; my first love, Daphne!

Narrator Two: And thus ends the happy/sad story of Daphne and Apollo. Sad, in that Cupid played a cruel joke which robbed them both of love, but happy, in that the laurel tree leaves have been used to crown heroes and scholars throughout the ages. Daphne would remain forever young and praised for her beauty for ages to come.

Work Space

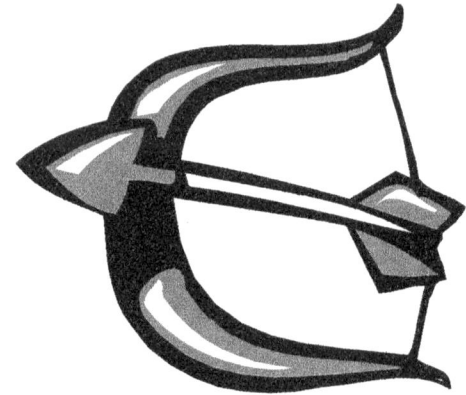

THE STORY OF DAPHNE AND APOLLO
Answers are on page 116

Putting It All Together

ODYSSEUS AND THE CYCLOPS

Reading Parts: Narrator One, Narrator Two, Odysseus (O-diss-ee-us), Polyphemus (Polly-fee mus), Greek soldier one, Greek soldier two

Work Space

(1) Narrator One: Odysseus (O-diss' ee-us), the great Greek King of Ithica, was on his way home from the long and bloody Trojan War. He and his brave Greek warriors had fought for 10 years to defeat the great kingdom of Troy. Many had died, but 6,230 soldiers survived. Odysseus was determined to get them home alive. He had 7 large sailing ships and knew that each ship would have to hold _____ men. It would be a long and dangerous trip. The men were getting very tired and food was running low.

(2) Odysseus: Cheer up men! Our look-out has spied a nearby island, where I hope to find food and fresh water for all. We will rest there for awhile to regain our strength. Our large ships cannot get close enough to the shore, but I want 936 men to use the 3 smaller boats and go ashore while the others wait here until we find out if this island is safe. The men quickly figured that there would be ___ men in each of the 3 boats.

(3) Narrator Two: When the three boats of Greek soldiers reached the strange island, they noticed a large cave, and entering it found pens of fat sheep, large stacks of cheese, and great buckets of milk. The men were near starvation and immediately began to eat. They remembered their hungry comrades on the ship and found three large bags to carry the 921 slabs of cheese they found. If evenly divided, each bag would hold _____ slabs.

(4) Odysseus: That's right men! Eat until you're full, and

© 2005 Polette, Ebbesmeyer 65 CLC0345 Pieces of Learning

ODYSSEUS AND THE CYCLOPS

then fill the sacks with food for our hungry men on the ships. Rest awhile until the owner of this cave returns. We must pay him for this fine food. He has numbered all the different foods in the Roman way of numbers. I can see he has 1(I) cask of wine and 2(II) barrels of oil. There are 3(III) buckets of milk and he has 5 crates of figs numbered by a V. Therefore the I in front of a V (IV) must stand for the number _____ and a 1 in back of a V (VI) stands for the number _____.

(5) Narrator One: The men were having a good time running around the cave to find the many different foods stored there and figuring out the Roman numerals. They counted 10 bunches of grapes and saw the (X) written there. So they figured (IX) would be ten minus 1, representing the number _____ and, therefore, 11 would be _____ in Roman numerals. They just had to add or subtract and by counting numbered objects, they learned that (L) stood for 50, (C) for 100 and (D) for 500. The men were enjoying themselves as they learned what numbers the letters stood for.

(6) Soldier One: Look, Demetrius! This guy must have an unbelievable appetite. He has 53 boxes of apples. There's the Roman numeral _____ right above them and here's the numeral _____ above the 34 boxes of figs.

(7) Soldier Two: You're right, Lucius. I can't imagine how

Work Space

ODYSSEUS AND THE CYCLOPS

one person could eat all this food. Think of all the meat he gets from 572 fat sheep. I saw the Roman Numeral _____ written right above their pens. And look here! He has 148 (Roman numeral) _____ bins of olives and 268 (Roman numeral) _____ oranges. I'm getting good at figuring out these Roman numerals, but we'd better get some of this food back to our men on the ships. This cave is beginning to give me the creeps.

(8) Odysseus: I'm proud of you, my brave soldiers. You've learned the Roman numeral system of numbers and I see you packing up the food for our fellow warriors. We can't wait much longer for our host; whomever he might be. But we will leave money for the provisions we have taken. Keep track of how much we take along. From what you've learned, you know that he has numbered his walnuts at (DCCLXVIII). If you pack up half of them, be sure to record the number _____ in our books for payment.

(9) Narrator Two: The men were anxious to get back to the ships. They quickly packed the food needed to continue their journey home. They recorded the following numbers for payment:

1/4 of (CCLXVIII) oranges = _____ oranges for payment
1/5 of (X) boxes of grapes = _____ boxes of grapes
1/2 of (CXLVIII) olives = _____ bins of olives
3/4 of (DLXXII) sheep = _____ sheep

Suddenly they stopped their work as they felt the ground tremble and saw a huge shadow fill the entrance to the cave. It was a hideous one-eyed monster standing there and roaring in a loud voice.

(10) Polyphemus: Who has dared to enter the home of

Work Space

ODYSSEUS AND THE CYCLOPS

the Cyclops, Polyphemus? And what are you doing with my food and my prized sheep? Don't you realize you have landed on the island of the Cyclops where there is no hope of escape? There are 6,659 of us and though 32 boats left this morning with 208 Cyclops in each boat, that leaves _____ of us to destroy the lot of you. I assure you, it will be an easy task for us!

(11) Odysseus: We are Greek soldiers, trying to get home from the Trojan war. We came here in peace asking only for some food and rest. We intend to pay for everything we use. Surely you will take pity on us, for we meant you no harm. The Trojan war was very long and expensive. But, of the 7,840 gold pieces we started with, we have 1/10 left. You can have all of the _____ gold pieces left, to use in any way you want.

(12) Polyphemus: What do I want of your silly gold pieces? I have all I need on this island. This cave is my home, and the sheep are my children. Did you really think you could buy them from me? You see from my sign that I have 572 of my beautiful animals. I started with only 1/4 that number. So, you see I only had _____ sheep in the beginning. I worked hard to build up this flock. It took a lot of time and care. I'm not about to let you have any of them!

(13) Odysseus: Be reasonable, my friend. I am the King

Work Space

ODYSSEUS AND THE CYCLOPS

of Ithica. I will reward you well for any help you give us. We need the meat of the sheep to live on. If you increased your 572 sheep from 1/4 that number at the beginning, you now have an increase of _____ sheep that you can share with us.

(14) Polyphemus: First of all, I'm not your friend! I'm your worst nightmare!! Haven't you wondered why my number of sheep keep increasing so rapidly? It's because I do not eat them. I will not share my sheep. Oh no! But *you* will share your men. For that is what I eat!! I have counted 936 men who have entered my cave. Now, put them into groups of 6 so that I might have 2 for breakfast, 2 for lunch and 2 for dinner I had better see _____ groups ready to be tied together when you are finished!

(15) Odysseus: Be reasonable, Cyclops. Surely you are jesting about eating my men. This is September. To eat 6 men a day, you would have to eat _____ this month; and in October _____ more. No one could eat that much!! I'm sure we can come to some agreement that will satisfy you and allow us to be on our way home. There is so much to eat, other than human flesh. Can we interest you in something more tasty? We will be glad to serve you vegetables and fruit for dinner tonight.

(16) Narrator One: The men watched in horror as the

Work Space

ODYSSEUS AND THE CYCLOPS

Work Space

monster Cyclops rolled a large stone to block the entrance, and grabbing two men, devoured them in a matter of seconds. He told the men that he would enjoy two more of them at his 7:15 breakfast. He then drank some wine and rolled over for a long night's sleep. Odysseus watched him carefully as he poured 2 pints from the gallon jug of wine. The jug had been full, so Odysseus knew there were _____ pints left. He was beginning to form a plan of escape from the hideous creature who held them prisoner.

(17) Soldier One: Odysseus, please save us! That monster means to kill every one of us. We're trapped in this cave with no way out! That stone he blocked the entrance with must weigh a 1 1/2 ton. Why that's _____ pounds. All of us together couldn't budge it. What are we going to do? Are we doomed to end up in this terrible cave of the Cyclops after we fought so long and hard to defeat the Trojans?

(18) Soldier Two: The monster said he had his breakfast at 7:15 A.M. It's 9:40 P.M. now. That gives us _____ hours ____ minutes to think of a way to escape. I, for one, think there is no hope! He is too strong and too evil for us. I honor you, Odysseus, King of Ithica, but I believe there is no way we can solve this deadly and dangerous problem.

(19) Odysseus: Take courage, Lucius! He has strength, and he has evil intent. But we have goodness on our side

ODYSSEUS AND THE CYCLOPS

and thinking minds that will aid us in solving this problem. I noted that it took 2 pints of wine to put him to sleep tonight. Tomorrow we will offer him 1 1/2 gallons of our own wine. He drinks it from the pint containers. So, be ready to have _____ pints ready. We will put him in a deep sleep and put out his only, evil eye with one of the huge logs that we will sharpen to a point and heat in the great fireplace. It is our only chance.

(20) Narrator Two: The men had very little sleep that night. They were bundled into groups of six and could think of nothing but what was going to happen when the Cyclops woke up for his breakfast. Two of the 936 soldiers were already gone. If their plan didn't work, in one more week they would lose _____ more of the warriors. It was a terrible thought. They knew they must act quickly.

(21) Odysseus: I know you brave men are worried about who of us will be gone by tomorrow. Counting the two we lost today, we will only have _____ men left in another week. We can't afford to lose those men. I have picked out the log that we will sharpen to a fine point. All of us will work on it and destroy this monster tomorrow night. Now try and get some rest. You will need it for what lies ahead.

(22) Narrator Two: The men had a right to be terrified. The next morning Polyphemus devoured two more men

Work Space

ODYSSEUS AND THE CYCLOPS

with his breakfast before leaving the cave with his sheep. He made sure he had all 572 sheep by putting them in groups of 10. This gave him _____ groups with _____ sheep left over. He promised to be home for lunch and laughed at their horrified faces as he resealed the entrance with the stone. The men looked to their leader for help. Odysseus had not brought them through the Trojan War to end up dying on the island of the Cyclops.

(23) Odysseus: All right men! If you don't want to die, get busy sharpening this large log to a fine point. We don't have too much time. It's 8:45 A.M. now. The Cyclops will be home for lunch at noon. He'll be gone again at 1 P.M. I'm sure he'll return at the same time he did yesterday - 6:30 P.M. That gives us _____ hours and _____ minutes. We can do it in that amount of time. So let's get busy!

(24) Narrator One: The men needed no more encouragement. They went to work, and the log was carved to a sharp point. At lunch, ten men sat on it to hide it from the monster. Polyphemus must have felt that something was going on because he stalked the whole perimeter of the rectangular cave. He did it over and over as he ate lunch. Being 45 feet long on both sides and 27 feet wide and by walking it 9 times, he had covered _____ feet. The men were relieved when he finally left and they could finish their job.

(25) Soldier One: We're finished, Odysseus. The log is sharpened and getting red-hot in the fire. The Cyclops

Work Space

ODYSSEUS AND THE CYCLOPS

should be home soon. I hope we can fill him with enough wine to put him to sleep before dinner. We don't want to lose any more men. We know he'll be back at 6:30 P.M. He left at 1 P.M. and he's been gone for 4 hours and 15 minutes, so he'll be back in _____ minutes. Let's be ready to talk him into drinking a lot of wine.

(26) Narrator Two: When the Cyclops returned, he was surprised to see many pints of wine set out for him. The warriors were offering the best wine they had carried from the ships. Poyphemus had never tasted such good wine and could not get enough of it. He added 4 pints to the 1 1/2 gallons on the table. In all, he drank _____ pints before he fell over in a deep sleep.

(27) Odysseus: Quick, men! Bring the log over here! Put out this evil eye while he sleeps. Then go to the sheep and crawl under them for our escape. The Cyclops will roll back the stone and leave with his sheep to get help from his fellow cyclops, but we will escape by traveling under the sheep as they leave the cave. There are 572 sheep and he ate 6 of the 936 men who entered here. So, _____ men will have to double up with someone under the sheep. They are big animals, so there will be room to hide two of you.

(28) Narrator One: It happened just as Odysseus had predicted. The warriors put out the evil eye and Poyphemus

Work Space

© 2005 Polette, Ebbesmeyer   73   CLC0345 Pieces of Learning

ODYSSEUS AND THE CYCLOPS

awoke, roaring with rage. He could not see, but he groped around the cave trying to find the Greek soldiers. He could find none for they were all hiding beneath the huge beasts. Most of them had to double under one sheep, but _____ men were hiding easily beneath a single, large sheep.

Narrator Two: Polyphemus knew he had to get help, so he rolled back the stone just far enough to squeeze through and let out one sheep at a time. He patted each one from head to tail. That way, he was sure none of the warriors could escape by riding the huge sheep. He intended that none of them would leave the cave alive. However, Odysseus tricked the monster by keeping his men *under* the animals and escaped with his men to the waiting ships. They sailed away as Polyphemus howled in rage and defeat. Goodness and quick thinking had won over evil!

Work Space

ODYSSEUS AND THE CYCLOPS
Answers are on pages 116 and 117

Putting It All Together

CEYX AND HALCYONE

Reading Parts: Narrator, Ceyx (seeks), Halcyone (hal-see' own-ee), Hera (here' ah), Somnus

Work Space

(1) Narrator: Ceyx (seeks) was the king of Thessaly and the husband of Halcyone (hal-see'-own-ee). They loved each other very much and could not bear to be apart. Of course, as king, he had to travel at times around the country. Halcyone kept track of the days he was away. In the past year, Ceyx had been gone 24 days at sea and 13 days traveling on land. She knew that he was gone _____ more days or _____ % when he traveled by sea.

(2) Ceyx: Halcyone, my dear wife, I know you hate the sea journeys I must take. I don't like them either, but I have many problems that have troubled me for too long. I must visit the oracle and get the advice I need. It is 3000 miles across the sea and the island of the oracle is 3/4 of the way. I must sail _____ miles to reach my destination. It will be a long trip!

(3) Halcyone: Dear husband, please do not go! I beg this of you!! It is not only a long journey, but a dangerous one. Last year there were 3,624 lives lost on ordinary trips at sea, but there were 5 times that number for those who journeyed to the oracle. Can you imagine _____ lives lost on that dangerous trip? If you must go, I beg you to take me along.

CEYX AND HALCYONE

(4) Ceyx: Oh no, dear wife! I will not lie to you about the danger of the trip. However, I refuse to put *your* life in any danger. Pray for my safe return, as you always do. It will take many more prayers than usual so spread them out throughout the day and night. I know you do not sleep while I am gone. If you say 4 prayers for every hour, there will be _____ petitions for my safety every day. Surely I will be safe from the wild and tossing waves of the sea.

(5) Narrator: Halcyone watched in misery as Ceyx and his ship sailed out to sea. She could only hope and pray for calm seas and a courageous crew to bring her husband back safely. What she didn't know was that 1/3 of the 648 crewmen had never sailed before. That was _____ crewmen who knew little about the raging storms that they would have to face. And the winds were already causing a violent storm for Ceyx and his men.

(6) Ceyx: Have courage, brave sailors! I have never seen the waves so high nor the wind so strong! I fear Poseidon (po-sigh-done) has plans to take us down to his watery kingdom. There will be no return, so hang on to the sail lines for your lives! 339 men have been washed overboard already! That leaves _____ to bring this ship to land and safety. Think of your loved ones waiting for you. Don't let Poseidon win this battle.

Work Space

CEYX AND HALCYONE

Work Space

(7) Narrator: The men tried bravely to battle the storm and keep the ship from sinking, but in the end, they lost. One by one the waves washed over them and they drowned. Ceyx called out Halcyone's name as a large wave covered him and he was carried down, 1,250 feet, then 1,345 feet more, and finally an additional _____ feet to bring him one mile deep. Ceyx knew he would never return to the land of the living again. His one regret was leaving his beloved, Halcyone.

(8) Halcyone: The days seem so long since Ceyx left me here, alone. I've prayed for hours for his safe return, but my heart tells me something is not right. Perhaps if I weave him a new robe, these sad thoughts will leave me for awhile. If I weave for 35 minutes every hour for 1/2 a day and 15 minutes for every hour the rest of the day, I'll be busy for _____ hours of each day. That should make the time seem to pass faster.

(9) Narrator: The gods on Mount Olympus felt sorry for Halcyone. She was praying every day, not knowing that her husband was already dead. They decided to visit her in a dream and tell her the truth about her husband's death. When Halcyone heard the message in her sleep, she cried for hours. Her tears would fill 2 1/2 cups, and so she lost _____ fluid ounces of moisture through her weeping as she ran down to the seashore. The gods decided she had sacrificed enough. They would find a way to reunite her with Ceyx!

CEYX AND HALCYONE

Work Space

(10) Halcyone: I cannot live without you, dear Ceyx! I *will* not live without you! I see the sun is coming up, and a new day is about to begin. I do not want to spend another day alone. You are out there in the sea, somewhere and I am a strong swimmer. I cannot swim over 2000 miles to the land of the oracle, but if I can swim 225 miles in between the many island and swim for _____ days, I may find you with the oracle.

Narrator: Halcyone threw herself into the sea. But she never even touched the water. Instead, she found herself flying over the waves. Her body had wings and she was covered in feathers. She had turned into a bird along with her husband. Together they flew over the sea, never to be parted again.

CEYX AND HALCYONE

Answers are on page 117

Putting It All Together

THE QUEEN OF THE DEAD

Reading Parts: Narrator One, Narrator Two, Persephone (per-sef o nee), Demeter (dem-a ter), Hades (hay deez), Apollo, Zeus

Work Space

(1) Narrator One: There was once a beautiful young maiden named Persephone. She was the daughter of the goddess Demeter who ruled the harvests of the earth. It was Demeter who taught Persephone about the months being evenly divided between winter and summer. There were 3 months of frigid weather, 2 months of cold and 1 month of moderating temperatures that made up the ___ months of winter.

(2) Demeter: During some seasons, the temperatures will vary, my daughter, and you'll see 1 frigid, 3 cold and 2 moderate months. But they always add up to the same number, no matter what the order. So you can figure 3+2+1 or (2+1) +3 or 2+ (1+3). No matter how you group the numbers to add, the sum, plus the number of summer months will always be _____.

(3) Persephone: Oh, Mother, I love to learn the different ways you can play with numbers. Last week was fun when we were counting the pumpkins that were ready for harvest. You tried to trick me by replacing numbers with letters. Remember how we recorded the 70 ripe pumpkins in the two fields as 27 (in field one) + "a" (in field two) = 70? You made me figure out that "a" was the variable that stood for the number _____.

© 2005 Polette, Ebbesmeyer

THE QUEEN OF THE DEAD

Work Space

(4) Demeter: Yes, dear daughter, I remember our fun with numbers. I must work with them at all times with the many things that must be recorded during the changing seasons. It helps to know that adding the months is related to subtracting them, because the two are opposite operations. I can solve the problem of supplying 75 sunny days to the farmers by knowing that I'll add 31 days in June to "n" numbers in May to equal 75. "n" = _____ .

(5) Persephone: And then you can check your addition by subtracting 31 from 75 to see if you get "n" number again. "n" = _____ . I think this is fun! Can I help you keep the records during the harvest seasons? I want to see how you divide the riches of the earth so that no one ever goes hungry. And how many seeds have to multiply to feed the ever-growing number of people.

(6) Demeter: I'm glad you like to help me solve the problems of feeding the world, Persephone. I will use your keen mind in many ways before long. But now I want you to enjoy this lovely day and gather flowers in the warm sunshine. You have worked every day for 276 days of this year. There are only _____ days left in this year. It's time to relax by the river for awhile.

THE QUEEN OF THE DEAD

Work Space

(7) Narrator Two: Persephone did as her mother asked her to do. She waved good-bye as she ran to the river to gather flowers. At the same time, Hades, god of the underworld, was driving his chariot near the river. He was tired because he had visited 192 towns, that day and interviewed 9 maidens in each town. He had talked to _____ young women in all trying to find a suitable queen for his underworld kingdom. Just as he was about to return home, he spied Persephone at the river bank.

(8) Hades: Stop horses! Stop!! That is the most beautiful maiden I have ever seen. I was about to give up on my search for a queen, but the gods have smiled on me and allowed me to find one who is worthy to share my kingdom. I have all the treasures of the ground. I will share them with her. Most gods think my treasures are in the millions, but actually, I have 10 hundred millions! How envious they would be if they realized I had _____ billion treasures.

(9) Narrator One: Persephone screamed in terror and called out to her mother when she saw Hades and his chariot bearing down on her at great speed. But by the time her cry was voiced, she was already gone, deep inside the earth to the Kingdom of the Dead! Down, down, down they went – 4,832 miles deep. Hades always rounded the number to _____ miles to make it seem deeper to those who feared him. It was deep enough to keep the cry for help from Demeter's ears, but the wind carried the plea for help to where she dwelled on Mount Olympus and sent her hurrying back, in fear, to the river where she had left her daughter.

© 2005 Polette, Ebbesmeyer   81   CLC0345 Pieces of Learning

THE QUEEN OF THE DEAD

Work Space

(10) Demeter: My dear daughter, what has happened to you? River! Wind! Animals! Tell me! Where is my daughter? Please answer me!! You owe me favors from the many times I have helped you throughout the year. River, you called on me 9.607 times to calm your turbulence. And Wind, you asked me for directions 3.23 times. And all you animals - there were 18.76 occasions when I aided you. All together that makes _____ times I answered your pleas. Will not one of you help me, now?

(11) Narrator Two: The River, Wind, and Animals added the numbers given them by Demeter. They rounded the number and realized she had come to their aid _____ times, but still they did not answer her, for they were afraid of Hades. Demeter was overcome with sadness and sat down by the river and cried.

(12) Demeter: I will stay here by the river forever if I must. This is where I last saw my beloved daughter. I dare not leave this spot in case she returns here. It seems impossible that only this morning I paid her for her week's work for me. She got $0.69 for every errand and this week she had run errands 9 times. What a good girl. She planned on giving part of her _____ earnings to the poor. Surely no harm will come to such a generous and lovely young girl!

THE QUEEN OF THE DEAD

Work Space

(13) Apollo: Demeter, you have sat here by the river for days and days. I have watched you from Mount Olympus. Your heartbroken crying has filled me with pity. I will tell you the truth, dear Demeter, so that your heart may heal. Your daughter, Persephone, is alive. Yet she lives among the dead. She was taken by Hades who made her his bride. She is the Queen of the underworld and no one escapes the underworld. Just yesterday, 100 spirits tried 2.345 times to escape back to earth. But none of the _____ attempts were successful. She is there to stay!

(14) Narrator One: The news made Demeter even more sorrowful. She could not bear to think of Persephone as the bride of Hades. The underworld was no place for her beautiful daughter, even though she *was* queen of a god. In her frustration and sadness, Demeter left Mount Olympus and lived on earth. Every 49.6 days, Apollo appealed for her return to Olympus. She refused his appeal 6.8 times and, therefore, remained on earth for _____ days. During this time all the people on earth suffered.

(15) Zeus: Demeter, you have forced me to leave Mount Olympus and that makes me angry. Can't you see what you are doing to the people on earth? You are the goddess of the harvest, and with your absence the seeds will not sprout, and the crops will not grow. The fruit dies on the vine. There are only 6,256 fruit trees left and 8 regions are asking for their yield. Each region will receive only _____ trees of fruit to feed thousands of people. They will surely starve. If you return, I will order Hades to return his bride.

(16) Narrator Two: Zeus *did* order Hades to give

THE QUEEN OF THE DEAD

Persephone back to her mother. But there was one condition. She could only come back if she had eaten nothing during her time in the underworld. Hades was very sad because he knew his bride had not eaten since being with him. She said the food was tasteless. Hades had tried every food he could think of in the 336.76 days that she had been with him. He had given 6 cooks an equal number of days to fix foods that might tempt her, but though this gave each of them _____ days, they all failed. Then Hades got an idea!

(17) Hades: I know what I can do to make Persephone eat some food with me! It's the fruit of earth that she misses. I know how hungry she must be by this time, so I must visit earth now and bring something back that she can't refuse. I think pomegranates are her favorite fruit, but the earth has little food left. I hear that 90% of the 2000 pomegranates are gone. I must hurry before the remaining _____ are eaten.

(18) Narrator One: Hades was successful in finding sweet-tasting pomegranates to bring back to his bride. He took all that was left on earth. Hades didn't care if the people on earth went without food. He was only interested in tricking his wife into eating something. When she saw the fruit, her appetite returned. She ate greedily for a week. The first day she ate 70 fruits, the second 30, the third day it was 25 and 15 on the fourth. The last three days, she had 13, 8, and 7. In one week Persephone had eaten a daily average of _____ pomegranates! Hades was jubilant!!

(19) Narrator One: When Persephone saw that only

Work Space

THE QUEEN OF THE DEAD

_____ pomegranates remained in the basket, she realized how she had been tricked. She sat down and cried bitterly. Hades was very upset to see his queen so sad. He decided to visit Zeus and work out some plan that would satisfy everyone.

(20) Zeus: Well Hades, have you come to tell me that Persephone is on her way back to her grieving mother? And that the world is blooming and budding again with a fruitful harvest? Do you realize the meat on earth has been depleted by 47%, the grain by 31% and the vegetables by 17%. That leaves only _____ % of edible foods to feed the starving people. I want to hear that you have solved this dilemma!!

(21) Hades: Oh great king of the universe, I come with a plan that I hope will make us all happy. I can see that Persephone needs to see her mother at times. However, she has also grown very fond of me. I love her dearly, Zeus. And I am willing to be very generous. All I ask is that she remain with me for 1/3 of the year. That way she will spend _____ months as Queen of the Underworld and _____ months with her mother. Surely that should please everyone.

Narrator One: Zeus was pleased with the plan that Hades

Work Space

THE QUEEN OF THE DEAD

Work Space

had devised. It seemed that Demeter and Persephone were satisfied with the compromise. And so it has been since that time. Each year when Persephone is with her mother, the earth is warm and green while the crops flourish. But when she returns to Hades in the Underworld, the fields are empty and the earth turns very cold. We call this time of year mid-winter.

THE QUEEN OF THE DEAD

Answers are on page 117

Putting It All Together

DAEDALUS, THE BIRD MAN

Reading Parts: Narrator One, Narrator Two, Daedalus (ded-a lus), King Minos, Icarus (ic-a rus)

Work Space

Narrator One: Daedalus was the most famous architect in the world. He became so well known because of the awesome labyrinth he designed and built for King Minos of Crete. The huge maze of criss-crossed paths were a source of amazement to everyone who heard about them. Powerful Kings vied for his services. They brought fame to anyone who was wealthy enough to hire him. In fact, the labyrinth had almost ruined King Minos financially.

(1) Minos: Daedalus, I am so proud of the magnificent labyrinth you have designed and built for me. However, my treasury is almost depleted. I have paid you everything but the last $825. Could I pay you $200 now and the rest of the cost in 5 equal monthly installments at 6% interest? The added interest each month of _____ will increase your total payment and the extra time would allow me to replenish my treasury.

(2) Daedalus: I appreciate your problem, Minos, but I would prefer to be paid in full at this time. I have plans to roam the world and discover new things with my son, Icarus. I'll tell you what I'll do! If you get the money and pay me in full, I'll give you a 7% discount on what you owe me. That way your payment will be reduced by _____. I'm sure you have wealthy friends who will help you raise the amount you owe me and I am very anxious to be on my way.

© 2005 Polette, Ebbesmeyer   87   CLC0345 Pieces of Learning

DAEDALUS, THE BIRD MAN

(3) Minos: It is generous of you to reduce my final payment to _____, by giving a 7% discount, but even that amount will be a hardship on me at this time. A kingdom of this size and importance takes a great deal of money to maintain. I have paid you great sums of money and I hope you will be reasonable. As for taking loans from my friends, I have no intention of letting them know my finances. I would be the object of ridicule in every kingdom of the world and no longer the most powerful ruler on earth!

(4) Narrator One: Daedalus could see that Minos was losing patience with him. But he was weary of this pompous King and not interested in waiting around for 5 months, even with 6% interest, to collect the monthly installment, amounting to $_____. He wanted to leave Crete and be free to exchange new ideas with many different people. However, he forgot how powerful King Minos was, and how he could punish those who thwarted him in any way. When he told Minos he was leaving Crete the next day, the King was furious and determined to teach Daedalus a lesson that would last a lifetime. He wanted everyone to know what happens to those who oppose the will of the king. He decided the punishment would be harsh.

Work Space

DAEDALUS, THE BIRD MAN

Work Space

(5) Minos: I tried to give you, in total, an extra _____ dollars and _____ cents by paying over five months at 6% interest, but you are selfishly insisting on demanding full payment at this time. You will leave Crete, all right. But not as you planned. You and your son will be banished to an island where there is no escape. You will be my prisoner forever. I hope you have many years to regret your actions against the mighty King Minos! In fact, I will make sure that you have the rest of your life to suffer regrets!

(6) Narrator Two: Daedalus was in shock at hearing what was going to happen to him and his son. He knew he had to think fast to find any means of escape, but there didn't seem to be any. The guards came quickly to take the two away. Daedalus had no idea where they were being taken. He knew it might be important to know how far they would travel. Being an engineer he knew that distance equals rate times time; so he listened closely when the guards talked of having to cover 20 miles an hour for the next 12 hours. Daedalus figured they were going _____ miles away. He wondered if they would ever know freedom again. His first concern was for his son.

DAEDALUS, THE BIRD MAN

Work Space

(7) Daedalus: Icarus, I'm afraid that I have put us in mortal danger because of the stupid way I treated the King. I should have made him a gift of the last payment and left Crete with his blessing instead of his curse. But now we're on our way to an island of no return. We have been gone for half the time it will take us to get there. It's now 10:30 P.M. We should reach the island by _____. I hope there's an early dawn, so we can look for any possible means of escape before we are taken up the high cliffs. This is the time to use all of our senses and miss no opportunity to find a way out of our predicament. Tell me every and all the ideas of escape that come to your mind.

(8) Icarus: Please don't blame yourself, Father. You were owed the money. You had a right to demand payment. Right is right! And even a king should have to abide by it. We have done nothing wrong. We will find a way to regain our freedom. You are such a creative thinker and always have 3 times as many good ideas as I do. Even if the two of us think of 48 good ideas, I know that only _____ of those ideas will be mine.

(9) Narrator One: Icarus was right! Daedalus *did* have 3 times as many good ideas as Icarus did on every subject. Daedalus knew full well that if the two of them had 48 good ideas _____ of the ideas would be his. But that's as it should be. He was the architect and engineer; he was the adult. He was the one who got them in this mess. Therefore, when they were put on the island, Daedalus spent every day on the beach, trying to create an idea for escape. One day, the idea came to him.

DAEDALUS, THE BIRD MAN

Work Space

(10) Daedalus: Icarus come quickly! I've thought of a way to get off this island! It is daring, but it just might work. First you must gather all the feathers the sea gulls have dropped on the island. I have watched them for days and noticed 400 dropped on Sunday, 550 on Monday, 425 Tuesday and 400 dropped the next four days in a row. So, every week they drop an average of _____ feathers a day on the island. That is good because I will need thousands of these feathers. Now get to work my son.

(11) Narrator Two: Icarus did as his father asked. For days and weeks he gathered huge piles of bird feathers and placed them near Daedalus as he fashioned two wooden frames shaped like birds' wings. Icarus began to understand what his father planned to do. Daedalus figured he needed 50,000 feathers. With the average number dropped every day, Icarus knew it would take him _____ days to collect that number. He was getting very excited as he thought of his father's plan. He just hoped it would be successful. At last the day came when both were finished with their work.

(12) Daedalus: Well, Icarus, it is time to try out our wings. You did a great job of collecting the bird feathers. Since I only used 2/3 of the 50,000 feathers, we have _____ of them left, in case we need to repair the wings at any time.

DAEDALUS, THE BIRD MAN

Work Space

(13) Narrator One: Daedalus inspected the wings to make sure the feathers had been glued on tightly with the tar they had found in the pits. He then strapped the wings on and ran off the edge of the cliff. He felt himself lifted into the breeze. The wings worked! Daedalus flew in a circle to return to the island. The circle had a diameter of 13 centimeters, so the circumference was about _____ centimeters. He landed to find his son very eager to try his wings and fly far away from the island prison.

(14) Icarus: Oh, Father, what a thrill to watch you soaring through the air. I can't wait to fly and be free of this place. I figure we are 86 kilometers from a friendly island. I'm sure we can fly 2 kilometers per minute. So we can reach freedom in _____ minutes.

(15) Daedalus: I know how anxious you are to leave this place, Icarus. But I caution you to remember my warnings. Do not fly too low and let your wings touch the water. It will pull you down. And do not fly too high, or the sun will burn your feathers. There is a lot of weight to lift. You and the wings together weigh 178 pounds. You weigh 3 times more than the wings, so you know you add _____ pounds to the wing weight. You will be safe if you follow me and do as I do. Now, let's catch the wind and take off!

DAEDALUS, THE BIRD MAN

Work Space

Narrator Two: The father and son caught the wind and flew from the island. But, as soon as Icarus felt himself flying, he forgot all the warnings. In sheer happiness he flew higher and higher, until the sun began to melt the glue that held the feathers to the frame. He called to his father for help, but Daedalus could do nothing but watch his son disappear into the sea. If only Icarus had listened to his father's advice!

DAEDALUS, THE BIRD MAN

Answers are on page 117

Putting It All Together

CHARIOT OF THE SUN

Reading Parts: Narrator One, Narrator Two, Helios (he-lee-os), Jupiter, Phaeton (fay-et-en), Clymene (klim-u-nee)

Work Space

(1) Narrator One: Helios, the sun god, had his gleaming palace high in the sky. He sat on a throne of emeralds, surrounded by his attendants, Day, Month, Year, Century, Hours, Spring, Summer, Autumn, and Winter. His radiance lit up the entire expanse of the sky. Mortals said he owned 10 billion sunbeams, but the truth was, he owned a trillion. So, instead of ten billion, he could shower the earth and sky with _____ billion beams of light. Each day he rode his fiery chariot drawn by four wild steeds, to bring the light of day to the earth below. All went well in the kingdom of the sun, until the day Helios was visited by his son Phaeton. The boy was born of a nymph named Clymene.

(2) Phaeton: Your brightness and the heat of your surroundings is almost blinding, Father! I've heard of your importance and of your power from my mother, Clymene, but your splendor and brilliance is overwhelming to my eyes. I was told your brightness would compare to the power of ten squared. How wrong to think of you as only one hundred times brighter. I would say your light is 10^6, which makes you _____ times brighter. I only wish I could raise my eyes to see you. I need to know if you are truly my father, and what proof you can give, if it is so. I have journeyed far to your palace so that everyone may know that Phaeton is the son of a great god!

CHARIOT OF THE SUN

(3) Helios: Welcome, my dear son, Phaeton! I will remove my radiant crown so that you can look upon me. Come and embrace your loving father. I gladly assure you that you are my son. If you seek proof, ask anything of me and I swear by the river Styx (sticks) to give you anything you ask! You will know how many wishes I will grant you, if you can evaluate this math expression. Show me what kind of mathematical thinker you are!

Evaluate $3x + 9xy - 10$, if $x = 3$ and $y = 7$. If you can do this, you'll know that I will grant you _____ wishes.

(4) Phaeton: You are very generous to offer me so many wishes to be granted, but I ask only one wish from you today. I want to drive your fiery chariot across the sky and turn night into day. I want to have the feeling of power that *you* possess and be able to laugh at the sky and shout to the earth below that *I* am the son of Helios and will prove my greatness. I know that being your son makes me only 1/2 as powerful as you, but today I hope to increase that 1/2 by 2/3 and then I'll be lacking only _____ of your ability. Then, and only then, will I feel the right to be called the son of Helios. No one will ever dare to laugh at me again.

Work Space

CHARIOT OF THE SUN

Work Space

(5) Helios: This is impossible, Phaeton! I am the only one of all the gods with the ability to control the horses along the steep and danger-filled path across the skies. I regret my oath and can only hope you will see how reckless it would be for you to even attempt such an impossible undertaking. You have no idea how dangerous it would be to think you could drive my winged horses through the fiery sky. Can you even read my map to figure out the distances you must travel? If the map scale reads 1 centimeter for every 50 kilometers actual distance, you must know the actual distance represented by 3.2 centimeters on the map would be _____. Otherwise, you will be hopelessly lost in the vast regions of the sky!

(6) Phaeton: Father, my wish is to drive the chariot of the sun across the sky. I will hold you to your promise. I realize how many measurements I must be able to calculate in order to stay on the middle path and neither go too high and burn the sky, nor too low and scorch the earth. I've studied the distances and know how quick my figuring must be if I calculate 6 x 2 feet 7 inches in order to miss the dangerous constellations or the animals of the zodiac. I will simply regroup inches as feet and know that after _____feet _____ inches, I must make a turn. Being your son, I will be able to handle these problems, so please place the golden rays on my head and rub the protecting ointment on my skin, for it is time to go!

CHARIOT OF THE SUN

Work Space

(7) Narrator Two: The goddess Dawn was coming quickly, getting ready to shine forth in all her crimson beauty. The moon and stars were hidden, and Helios knew it was time for the fiery chariot to make its journey across the sky. He stepped out of the palace with his son at his side and saw the gleaming cart with its tires of gold and silver and encrusted with every jewel imaginable, sparkling in the new morning. A great feeling of power filled Phaeton as he leaped into the chariot. Helios sadly cried out one last bit of advice, telling his son he had only 0.3 hours before the first turn, so in _____ minutes he had to guide the horses firmly to keep them from veering off the path. Phaeton was so filled with joy, he barely heard his father's last warning.

(8) Phaeton: Poor Father! Doesn't he know that I am young and strong enough to keep these fiery steeds under control? I have the map sealed to the spot in front of me. My teachers have taught me well in mathematical calculations. I have the courage, the strength and the brain power to succeed in this endeavor. No one will ever again question who my father is. But now, I must keep my eyes on the map and be ready to avoid the many hazards of the journey. I see where Helios has marked the distance of 200,000 meters to the northern bear. So, when I have traveled _____ kilometers, I'd better be ready to avoid that lumbering animal.

CHARIOT OF THE SUN

(9) Narrator One: Phaeton could not believe the speed at which he was being carried by the winged horses. He tried to watch as their sharp hooves ripped through the clouds. They flew higher and higher into the sky. There was barely time to heed the many instructions he had received from Helios. Phaeton knew the trip would be an exceedingly fast one and decided to record it in minutes, rather than hours. After 2 1/3 hours, he noted a total of _____ minutes had passed and wrote it in his record book. But when he loosened the reins to write, disaster struck.

(10) Jupiter: Great thunderbolts! What is happening to the earth and sky? I see the chariot of the sun tossed around like a leaf in the wind. A boy is trying to do what only Helios can accomplish. The horses are on the wrong path. The heavens are in a turmoil. Even the animals of the zodiac are in a rage. What madness came over Helios to allow the destruction I see? The heavens and earth are crying out in terror as flames spread over moon and stars, mountains and woodlands alike! It looks like 2/5 of the earth is already destroyed. I'll have to act quickly to save the remaining _____%. Only my thunderbolt, can stop that chariot!

Work Space

CHARIOT OF THE SUN

Work Space

(11) Narrator Two: Jupiter's bolt flew through the air and struck Phaeton, who still clung to the runaway chariot. Phaeton fell from 6000 feet in the air. Jupiter watched as he dropped 1/2 the distance, but turned away for the next 2/3 of the descent. It was then, when there was only _____ feet left to fall that Clymene saw her son reach his end in the river Po. The terrible fires on earth stopped burning, the animals of the zodiac settled down, and the heavens returned to their normal state. But Phaeton was dead, leaving Helios and Clymene to grieve their lost son.

(12) Clymene: Oh mighty Jupiter, I cannot bear the sorrow that fills my heart. My brave, handsome son lies dead in the river and my daughters and I are left in a world consumed by sadness. Life holds no more joy for us as we watch my sisters, the river nymphs, bathing his burned and broken body. His conduct was very reckless in trying to be the sun, but his courage was greater. In ratio, if his recklessness is as 7 is to 10, he would have 3 times that proportion in courage, as _____ is to _____. Please do not punish us for his bravery, but instead, find a way to comfort us in our grief.

(13) Narrator One: Jupiter took pity on Clymene and

CHARIOT OF THE SUN

Phaeton's sisters as he watched them bury the boy's body on the banks of the river Po. He changed them into poplar trees covered with beautiful golden leaves. The leaves were amber tears that dropped, at first in great abundance, because of their terrible grief. The leaves began to clog the river and impede the normal flow. Jupiter told the trees they could remain close to the river and their beloved Phaeton if they would lessen their weeping. Clymene decreased the 18 amber leaves she shed every second by 35%, bringing the number to _____. But there were still too many leaves falling!

(14) Clymene: I know of your great sadness, my dear daughters, but we must cooperate with Jupiter or he will deny us the comfort of being near our son and brother, Phaeton. I've watched your falling tears and counted 21 for every second. I beg of you to decrease them by 45% and bring that number to _____. I believe that will solve the river problem and appease the powerful Jupiter. The important thing is to remain here, where we can watch Helios drive his fiery chariot, bringing the bright morning son to our beautiful earth. It will shine on Phaeton's grave and remind us of his moment of joy and glory.

Work Space

CHARIOT OF THE SUN
Answers are on page 117

Putting It All Together

ATHENA AND THE WEAVING CONTEST

Reading Parts: Narrator One, Narrator Two, Athena, Arachne (uh-rack-nee), Old Woman, Wood Nymph, River Nymph

Work Space

(1) Narrator One: Arachne was a simple peasant girl who would have lived out her life with little notice, except for one unusual and skillful talent she possessed. Arachne could weave cloth like no other in the land. The wood and river nymphs would travel far and stand in awe at what she produced on her loom. The long threads of wool were dyed in brilliant hues and seemed to take on a life of their own as Arachne's fingers formed intricate designs.

She never seemed to tire of her creations. She worked 7 hours and 25 minutes every day and at the end of the week, Arachne knew her total time of _____ hours and _____ minutes had been spent in creating beauty! As the days went by, the crowd of people increased around the cottage. Her reputation spread to every corner of the land and was finally noted by the gods on Mount Olympus.

(2) Wood Nymph: Your cloth and colors are exceptionally beautiful today, Arachne. But it is your intricate patterns that are so amazing. I see how you follow your pattern book to create with great precision. I notice you have 5,627 flowers to place in each of 4,338 places in this tapestry. Knowing that 8 ones x 5= _____, 3 tens x 5 = _____, 3 hundreds x 5 =_____ and add the 4 thousands x 5 equaling _____ , I can see you'll have more than _____ million flowers to place in your tapestry. How do you do it? It must be a gift from Athena! Only a goddess could take common cloth and colors to create the unique designs you weave day after day. You must make an offering to thank her for this wonderful gift!

© 2005 Polette, Ebbesmeyer 101 CLC0345 Pieces of Learning

ATHENA AND THE WEAVING CONTEST

Work Space

(3) Arachne: Don't be ridiculous! Athena has nothing to do with my skill as a weaver. In fact, I could teach her a thing or two about beauty and weaving! I am the best because I have worked long and hard to master the art. I have stayed up many nights to work out the calculations for my patterns. You must be precise to the smallest fraction, to be the best. It starts simply with seeing patterns like 4.73—4.731—4.732—4.733—4.734—_____

_____—_____—_____—_____—_____—_____. But to be as good as I am, you must be able to do difficult calculations. I doubt that Athena could match my ability.

(4) River Nymph: Arachne, you must never think you are higher than the gods of Mount Olympus. And saying it out loud is asking for more trouble than any mortal can handle. I can see that you are very adept with figures, so keep in mind that your few problems in life, that might amount to 0.026 could quickly multiply a thousand times to _____ very difficult hardships, if Athena decides to punish you for your reckless words of insult. I beg of you to take back your hasty boast and ask forgiveness from Athena before it is too late. I must go now for I hear someone knocking at your door.

ATHENA AND THE WEAVING CONTEST

(5) Old Woman: Open the door, you silly girl, and listen to the advice I have to give you. I heard you compare yourself to the great goddess, Athena, and I'm here to warn you of the consequences for such foolish pride. The river nymph said your troubles could multiply a thousand times with Athena's intervention, but I'm here to tell you your few 0.026 troubles will increase 1,000,000 times to _____. Your troubles will multiply more quickly than the leaves on the trees and remain with you for the rest of your life! Why can't you be content to be the best among the mortals? You are tempting fate when you put yourself above those who live on Mount Olympus. There will be a price to pay!

(6) Arachne: What are you babbling about, you silly old woman! I don't want your advice, and I don't need it. People from far and near come to see my lovely tapestries and watch me weave my intricate patterns. They marvel at my math ability when I record how many of the 23 gold threads I'll use on the 4 sides of my tapestry and how many will be left to use again. I always record my answer as the whole number _____ remainder _____, as a mixed number _____, and as a decimal _____. So you see, old hag, Athena needs to come and learn something from *me*!

Work Space

ATHENA AND THE WEAVING CONTEST

Work Space

(7) Narrator Two: As soon as Arachne said the insulting words, a blinding light appeared with Athena in the middle of it. She had been the old woman in disguise and had tried to influence Arachne to change her arrogant ways, but Arachne would not back down; not even to a goddess! Athena now realized that if she had 830.7 reasons for Arachne to change and tried on 13 separate visits, giving the girl _____ different causes to be more humble, she would still fail. She decided to teach Arachne a lesson she would never forget!

(8) Athena: It's obvious you are determined to compete against me, Arachne. I have given you every chance to ask forgiveness and change your foolish ways. You will have the contest you have insisted on, and we will see who comes out the winner. I want the whole world to know, so your tapestries that are always six ft. long, will be 6 times 6 feet 8 inches long for the contest. I think that length of _____ will be enough for all to see. Go, you wood and river nymphs. Tell everyone to come and witness the contest between the peasant girl Arachne and the goddess Athena. All mortals must learn a lesson from what happens here today!

ATHENA AND THE WEAVING CONTEST

(9) Narrator One: The looms were rapidly set up for the two weavers as nymphs and mortals crowded around to watch. The two set to work without a minute's hesitation. It wasn't long before the brilliant colors of the threads were woven into magnificent pictures, patterns, and borders of gold, crimson, pinks, and purple. Those who watched were mesmerized by the dazzling scenes unfolding on the tapestries. The day wore on, and no one left their place. Food and drink were brought in for everyone. Chicken and hams, cooked vegetables, and fruit were all consumed. In addition, servants brought in 7 gallons and 1 quart of sweet cider. The crowd drank 4 gallons and 3 quarts before the remaining _____ gallons and _____ quarts of cider were poured down the drain. The contest was over! Everyone gathered to see the results.

(10) Arachne: Well, Athena, your tapestry showing the twelve greatest gods and goddesses on Mount Olympus is very impressive. However, you can see from the crowd admiring *my* tapestry with such awe and approval, that I am clearly the winner of the competition. I must thank you for insisting on such a long tapestry. Usually I get $25.28 for a 1-foot tapestry, but today I'll receive _____ for the 2.5-foot tapestry. I already have a buyer, so I'll just say good-bye and be on my way. I'm sure you are anxious to get back to Mount Olympus and forget this humiliating day as quickly as you can.

Work Space

ATHENA AND THE WEAVING CONTEST

Work Space

(11) Athena: You are a vain girl, Arachne! You are right about today's contest. Your craftsmanship is flawless. This has led you to think you know everything. And that is *so* untrue! You don't even know how to charge for your work. A tapestry of this kind should be worth $85, and you have forgotten the 6 3/4% tax charge that should be added. Your sale today should have amounted to _____. You cheated yourself, but the worst thing you did was to insult a goddess! You expect a reward for winning- and you will receive one. It will be one you will never forget!

(12) Narrator Two: As Athena spoke the harsh words to Arachne, the peasant girl felt a terrible change coming over her whole being. Athena was saying that Arachne's reward would ensure her to be the most famous of weavers for all time. Her children and her children's children would have the same reward. Meanwhile, Arachne's arms and legs began to shrivel up. Her head was growing smaller. Her body changed in shape. She watched in horror as she saw her eight hairy legs protruding from it. Athena had changed her into a spider! Arachne scurried away to weave her first magnificent web.

ATHENA AND THE WEAVING CONTEST
Answers are on page 118

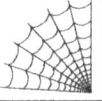

Putting It All Together

THE MAGNIFICENT MAZE OF MINOS

Reading Parts: Narrator One, Narrator Two, Minos (my-nose), Daedalus (dead-al-us), Theseus (thee-see-us), Aegeus (i-gee-us) Ariadne (ar-ee-ad-nee)

Work Space

(1) Narrator One: King Minos and his queen ruled the beautiful island of Crete, across the sea from the great Greek islands. The king wanted his queen to have a palace as splendid as her father's, the sun-god, Helios. To find a builder worthy of erecting such a mansion, the King held a contest for all applicants. There were many questions about stress, measurements, and materials, but the answer that won the competition told how many thrones could be made from 2 bars of gold if each throne called for the use of 2/3 of the gold bar. Minos looked at the answer _____ and knew it had been figured out by Daedalus, the greatest of the architects and engineers. He was delighted!

(2) Minos: You are the chosen one, Daedalus! You will use your unusual skills to build my queen a magnificent palace that will be known throughout the earth. In return, I will make you a wealthy man and a craftsman who will be renowned above all others. Spare no expense when you create this royal home. I have set aside $1,000,000 for the palace. I know that 1/2 of that will go for materials and 2/3 of what is left will be spent on furnishings. But you will still have $_____ to spend on decorations, paintings and frescoes that will make me the envy of all kingdoms. They will come from miles around to see the tall columns, winding stairs and great halls of my palace. Please start immediately. I can't wait to see the finished result!

(3) Narrator Two: The great palace of Cnossus (nos-

© 2005 Polette, Ebbesmeyer

THE MAGNIFICENT MAZE OF MINOS

sus) was completed and proved to be grander and more radiant than Minos had hoped for. The king and his court lived there in happiness until the time he angered Poseidon, the god of the sea. Minos tried to ask forgiveness. He sent a message down the 500 fathoms to Poseidon's underwater kingdom. He knew it took 1 minute to travel 5 feet so the message would take _____ hours to reach Poseidon. He waited in the palace for an answer of forgiveness, but instead he received a monster! It was half man, half bull, and ate nothing but human flesh. It was a disaster! The monster could not be allowed to roam free and eat whomever he pleased. Minos would have to enlist the help of Daedalus.

(4) Daedalus: I realize the great danger the whole kingdom is in, King Minos. Your entire population of 21,000 could all be devoured in a very short time! If you had to feed the monster 10 people twice a day, it would take only _____ weeks to deplete your entire population. I will construct a labyrinth under your whole palace to hold the evil beast. It will consist of a maze of twisted and turning passageways from which no one could find his way out. That will take care of keeping the animal enclosed, but *you* must find the humans to feed it!

(5) Minos: The monster is called the Minotaur, Daedalus,

Work Space

THE MAGNIFICENT MAZE OF MINOS

and your labyrinth is a unique idea for saving us! I will never be able to repay you. As for the human feedings, I will use the prisoners from the wars we fight. I have 32,000 prisoners in my camp. If I fed 20 a day for 3 years, I'd still have _____ prisoners left! To make sure I don't run out of victims before I find a way to destroy the Minotaur, I have threatened Aegeus, the King of Athens, with annihilation unless he sends fourteen Athenian youths to add to the victims. He has no choice, but to send them!

(6) Narrator One: Back in Athens, the King was sadly giving orders to ready the ship for sailing. It would carry the fourteen splendid young people to Crete and certain death. He thought that nothing could ever bring him happiness again. But on that day, a young man, named Theseus, was presented at court. He had come from far away, proclaiming to be the King's son. Theseus had traveled 2300 miles or _____ kilometers after hearing from his mother of the trouble in Crete. The King, who had once thought himself childless, was overjoyed to find that the young man, Theseus, was truly his son from a former marriage.

(7) Theseus: Father, I bring you the sword you buried so

THE MAGNIFICENT MAZE OF MINOS

Work Space

long ago beneath the stone. Only the son of the King would be strong enough to move the stone and therefore proof of whom I really am. The stone weighed 1000 pounds, or in your system of measurement _____ kilograms. No ordinary man could lift that weight. I am proud to be your son. I'm ready to find a way to destroy the Minotaur. This evil must stop, so I will be one of the fourteen young people on the ship that sails to Crete tomorrow! I do not seek to be the heir to the throne, so much as I seek to save your people from the monstrous beast and make you proud to claim me as your son.

(8) Aegeus: You are my true son, in every respect, Theseus! I admire your loyalty and courage, but I cannot bear to think of losing you just when I've found you again. I wish I could convince you to change your mind about going to Crete. I fear you have little idea of what a monster you will face. But since you are determined to go, take 2 identical triangular-shaped sails, one black and one white. Signal a safe return by hoisting the white sail in front of the black sail. Because the two sails are identical, we can say they are _____. Seeing the white sail will let me know that you are safe and the beast is dead! Go now with my blessing.

(9) Narrator Two: The ship sailed to Crete with seven

THE MAGNIFICENT MAZE OF MINOS

Work Space

young maidens and seven handsome youths. It was an expensive trip. Theseus saw the King pay the captain $1237.60 in tax money. Theseus knew the fee was rated at 5.6% of the King's yearly income, meaning the income this year was _____. Theseus was determined his father would get his money's worth from this trip by seeing the young Athenians returned alive and knowing the Minotaur would no longer be a menace to the great kingdom of Greece. What Theseus did *not* count on was meeting the beautiful princess Ariadne when they arrived in Crete. She was the loveliest maiden he had ever seen. He could not take his eyes from her. She, in turn, could not bear the thought of this handsome youth being torn apart by the evil Minotaur.

(10) Ariadne: Oh Theseus, I cannot bear to think of what will happen to you in the maze of paths so confusing that no one ever finds their way out again. I have begged Daedalus for his help. Being the designer of the labyrinth, he is the only one to know the way into the chamber of the Minotaur and the way to escape. I had to pay him dearly, but he agreed to give me a magic ball of thread which will roll out in front to lead you to the monster's chamber and back again to safety. You must surprise him in the middle of the night. We know how long he sleeps from recording when his terrible roaring stops and when it starts again. I counted the hours each night for a week. They were 12, 10, 11, 9, 12, 9 and 12. So you know the mean or average hours of his sleep are _____ hours. You must be in his chamber in half that time to insure surprise. But how will you kill him???

(11) Theseus: Don't worry, Ariadne. I have my father's

THE MAGNIFICENT MAZE OF MINOS

sword. If I was strong enough to lift the stone to retrieve it, I will be strong enough to thrust it into the monster. I practiced with the sword by killing dangerous animals in my homeland. I started with the smallest animal and after six times, I destroyed a very large wild animal. From first to last, the thrusts I needed to kill them were, 2, 4, 5, 7, 8, 10. So I know the median of this set of numbers is _____. I must be ready to thrust, at least that many times, to destroy the Minotaur. You have helped me beyond measure and you will be rewarded!

(12) Narrator One: In the dark of night, four and a half hours after the Minotaur had stopped roaring and gone to sleep, Ariadne led Theseus to the entrance of the labyrinth. She tied the end of the thread to the gate and gave the ball to Theseus. As soon as he put it on the ground, it rolled into the maze and he followed through twisting passageways, up and down stairs and into many dark hallways. At last he reached the chamber of the beast. He entered a room filled with a terrible stench and horrific snoring sounds. The room was, strangely, in the shape of a triangle. Theseus saw that the sides of the triangular walls were all of equal length, so it was shaped as an _____ triangle. Suddenly, he had no more time for observation, as the monster awoke and roared in rage and surprise.

Narrator Two: Theseus used the element of surprise to

Work Space

THE MAGNIFICENT MAZE OF MINOS

spring at the Minotaur and thrust his long sword into the cruel beast. It took seven thrusts to destroy the Minotaur and Theseus was depleted of strength. He barely made it out of the maze, where Ariadne waited for him. They rushed to the ship with the other Athenians and set sail for home. Ariadne went with them and, with the death of the beast, the trip was a success. However, there were sad results as well. Theseus abandoned Ariadne on an island and then forgot to change the black sails to white. His father, thinking Theseus was dead, jumped into the sea. However, Theseus lived to rule the kingdom and he named the sea after his father. We call it the Aegean Sea to this day!

THE MAGNIFICENT MAZE OF MINOS
Answers are on page 118

Work Space

ANSWERS

The Wolf, the Nanny Goat, and The Kid
Page 9
1. 5 bags
2. 36 miles
3. 35 minutes
4. 74 strawberries
5. 19 knocks
6. 6 hours
7. 9 windows
8. 30 minutes
9. 50 feet

The Milkmaid and Her Pail
Page 11
1. 277 steps
2. $5.99; $6.00
3. 145 chickens
4. 27 animals
5. $115.00
6. $45.00

The Man, the Boy and the Donkey
Page 13
1. 11 miles
2. 103 pounds
3. $31.55
4. 7 inches

The Lion and the Mouse
Page 14
1. 89 feet
2. $16.00
3. 36 pounds
4. 6 teeth
5. 51 seeds
6. 92 pounds
7. $380.00
8. 80 mice

Belling the Cat
Page 16
1. 45 mice
2. 461 mice
3. 431 mice
4. 9 hours
5. 162 minutes
6. 25 mice
7. 24 mice
8. 412 mice
9. 16 miles
10. 41 feet

The Hare and the Tortoise
Page 19
1. 18 minutes
2. 9 minutes
3. less than
4. 204 yards
5. will not
6. 4,710 strawberries
7. 112 pounds
8. 480 strawberries

The Fox and the Goat
Page 21
1. 104 heads of lettuce
2. 368 feet
3. 8000 bricks
4. 480 gallons

The Grasshopper and the Ants
Page 23
1. 126 seeds
2. 84 minutes
3. 84 hours
4. 92 days (counting 8/1 and 10/31)
5. $7.20
6. 48 inches
7. 3600 seeds
8. 32,934 seeds

The Boy Who Cried Wolf
Page 25
1. 40 sheep
2. $67.00
3. 4 hours
4. $37.00
5. 340 pounds
6. 4 villagers
7. 4 inches
8. 4 minutes

ANSWERS

The Town Mouse and the Country Mouse
Page 27
1. 12 visitors
2. 12 pieces
3. 27 mice
4. 80 cents
5. $52.00
6. 16 trips
7. $25.00

A Wolf in Sheep's Clothing
Page 29
1. 50 cents, $5,750
2. $1,500
3. $7,250
4. 25 days
5. 805 pounds
6. 6 barrels
7. 50 quarts
8. 34 sheep
9. 1 hour

Cinderella
Page 32
1. odd
2. $51.84 plus tax
3. $15.25
3. 1750 bricks
5. 6 hours
6. $2.25
7. $35.00
8. 6 hours
9. 10 days
10. $25,000
11. 5 hours
12. 24 dancers
13. 3 hours 30 minutes (if they rest after the last dance)
14. 180 minutes
15. 648 feet
16. 128 ounces
17. 168 hours
18. $9,125 (not including one or more leap years)
19. 1,000 years

The Golden Goose
Page 36
1. 391 square feet
2. 3 hours
3. 5 minutes
4. 28 hours
5. $216
6. 24 trees, 2 trees
7. 85 cents
8. 8 slices
9. 277 steps
10. $964
11. $15.00
12. 634 pounds
13. $51.84 plus tax
14. 2,136 miles
15. $5,450

The Tower of the Dragon
Page 39
1. 3/8
2. 234 feet
3. 181 miles
4. $62.50
5. $60.00
6. 2 ½ hours
7. 167 ¼ feet
8. 15 minutes
9. right
10. 240 minutes
11. 250 hours
12. 2,240 pieces
13. 16,500
14. 262 ½ seconds
15. can
16. 3 hours
17. $27/$108
18. 120 days or 121 if a leapyear
19. 90 hours
20. 14,400 pearls
21. 25 guests
22. 10 years
23. $266,666.66
24. 68 ½ years

ANSWERS

Hansel and Gretel
Page 45
1. 13 ½ miles
2. ½ cup
3. 2/7
4. 123 ¼ feet
5. 36 crumbs
6. 5 cords
7. 6 ½ hours
8. 5 6/16 or 5 3/8 inches
9. 58 loaves
10. 6 ¾ yards
11. 22 5/8 inches
12. 4 1/8 pounds
13. 14 ½ loaves
14. 2 quarts
15. 35 5/16 inches
16. 8 quarts
17. 1 ¼ hours
18. 24 cupcakes
19. 1,008 1/8 square inches
20. 82 pounds
21. 15 miles
22. 5 4/9 miles
23. ½ acre

The Fisherman and His Wife
Page 50
1. 38.4 pounds
2. 33%
3. $1,339.00
4. 551.54 yards
5. 1.2
6. 3.846 inches
7. 3,168
8. $4.66
9. $15.00
10. 47.52 miles per hour
11. 266.68 square yards
12. 1,209.8 miles

HERMES, THE MERRY OLYMPIAN
Page 54
1. 43 minutes
2. 17 minutes
3. 50 cows
4. 6 pieces
5. 22 minutes
6. 1000-100-10
7. $2,275
8. 10 percent
9. 8,000 bolts
10. 1 hour
11. 12 ideas
12. 389 melodies
13. 264 tunes
14. 108,000 wishes

THE STORY OF DAPHNE AND APOLLO
Page 59
1. 54,186,658 arrows
2. 5,950,249 golden and plain
3. 5,421,401 lead arrows
4. 13,637,744 arrows
5. 8 million arrows
6. 165 arrows
7. 77-75 trees
8. 5 boats – 3 nymphs
9. 311 minutes
10. 3/8 woods
11. $270.33
12. 2/4 or ½ chance
13. 26,400 feet
14. 2640 feet
15. 39,600 feet
16. 3,000 meters
17. 3 ¾ inches

ODYSSEUS AND THE CYCLOPS
Page 65
1. 890 men
2. 312 men
3. 307 slabs
4. 4, 6
5. 9, XI
6. LIII, XXXIV

ANSWERS

7. DLXXII, CXLVIII, CCLXVIII
8. 384
9. 67 oranges, 2 boxes, 74 bins, 429 sheep
10. 3 men
11. 784 gold pieces
12. 143 sheep
13. 429 sheep
14. 156 groups
15. 180 men, 186 men
16. 6 pints
17. 3,000 pounds
18. 9 hours 35 minutes
19. 12 pints
20. 42 warriors
21. 892 men
22. 57 groups, 2 sheep
23. 8 hours, 45 minutes
24. 1,296 feet
25. 75 minutes
26. 16 pints
27. 358 men
28. 214 men

CEYX AND HALCYONE
Page 75
1. 11 days or 54%
2. 2,250 miles
3. 18,120 lives
4. 96 petitions
5. 216 crewmen
6. 309 men
7. 2,685 feet
8. 10 hours
9. 20 fluid ounces
10. 10 days

THE QUEEN OF THE DEAD
Page 79
1. 6 months
2. 12
3. 43
4. 44
5. 44
6. 89 days
7. 1,728 young women
8. one
9. 5,000 miles

10. 31.597 times
11. 32 times
12. $6.21
13. 234.5 attempts
14. 337.28 days
15. 782 trees
16. 56.12 days
17. 200 pomegranates
18. 24 pomegranates
19. 32 pomegranates
20. 5%
21. 4 - 8 months

DAEDALUS, THE BIRD MAN
Page 87
1. $37.50
2. $57.75
3. $767.25
4. $132.50
5. $107.50
6. 240 miles
7. 4:30 A.M.
8. 12 ideas
9. 36 ideas
10. 425 feathers
11. 118 days
12. 16,667 feathers
13. 40.8 centimeters
14. 43 minutes
15. 133.5 pounds

CHARIOT OF THE SUN
Page 94
1. 10 hundred or 1000
2. 1,000,000 times
3. 188 wishes
4. 1/6 of your ability
5. 160 kilometers
6. 15 feet 6 inches
7. 18 minutes
8. 200 kilometers
9. 140 minutes
10. 60%
11. 1,000 feet
12. 21:30
13. 11.70 leaves
14. 11.55 tears

ANSWERS

ATHENA AND THE WEAVING CONTEST
Page 101
1. 51 hours and 55 minutes
2. 40-150-1,500-20,000; 24 million
3. 4.735—4.736—4.737—4.738—4.739—4.74
4. 26 problems
5. 26,000 problems
6. 5 remainder 3; 5 ¾; 5.75
7. 63.9 causes
8. 40 feet
9. 2 gallons; 2 quarts
10. $63.20
11. $90.74

THE MAGNIFICENT MAZE OF MINOS
Page 107
1. 3 thrones
2. $166,667
3. 10 hours
4. 150 weeks
5. 10,100 prisoners
6. 1,428.3 kilometers
7. 453 kilograms
8. congruent
9. $22,100
10. 10.7 hours
11. 6
12. equilateral

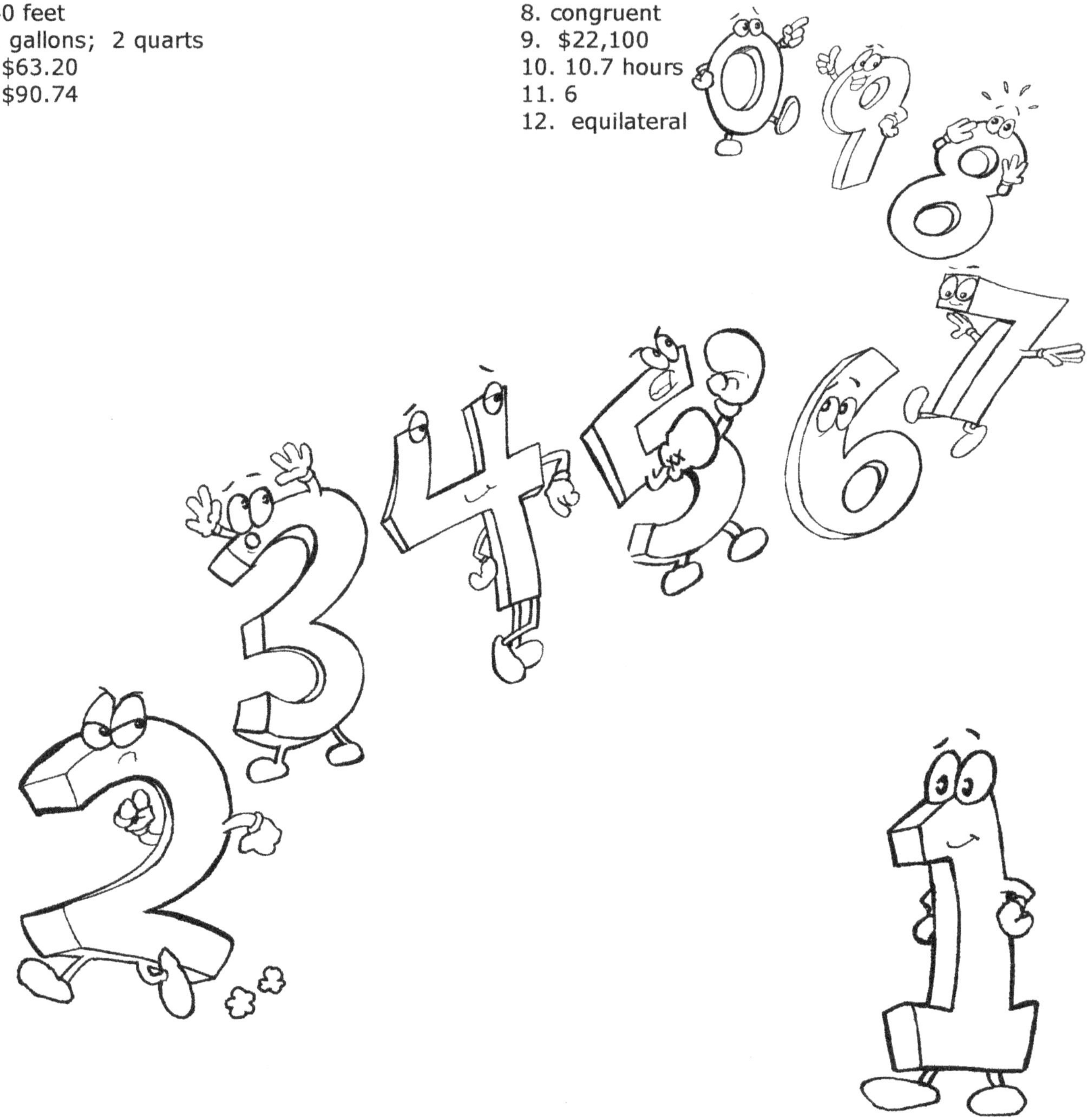